Good with
MONEY

Good with
MONEY

8 SIMPLE STEPS TO DITCH YOUR DEBTS, GROW YOUR SAVINGS AND LIVE YOUR BEST LIFE

LISA DUDSON

upstart press

A catalogue record for this book is available from the National Library of New Zealand.

ISBN 978-1-990003-87-5

An Upstart Press Book
Published in 2023 by Upstart Press Ltd
26 Greenpark Road, Penrose, Auckland 1061, New Zealand

Commissioning editor: Alison Brook
Editor: Brian O'Flaherty
Cover and text designed by Nick Turzynski, redinc. book design, www.redinc.co.nz

Printed by Dongguan P&C Printing Technology Co., Ltd.

Contents

Introduction

BEING GOOD WITH MONEY CAN MAKE a huge difference to your life and well-being. Not everything is about money, but it does make things a lot easier.

For as long as I can remember I've been good with my money. I grew up in a family that had to work very hard to have a basic lifestyle. There was never any spare money, but my parents did a great job of stretching it as far as possible, and I didn't necessarily want for anything. However, I did want to create a more financially comfortable lifestyle for myself. I had many jobs while I was young — three during high school at the same time — and I saved hard and learnt to be smart with my money. I'm not saying I haven't made some poor decisions over the years. Fortunately, on balance most of my decisions have been good!

I purchased my first shares in the New Zealand sharemarket when I was only 16 and developed a strong interest in personal finance and investing. So much so that in my late twenties, after my first career in IT, I became a financial advisor and have been advising clients since. Along the way I have learnt a lot and have long lost count of how many books I have read and courses and events I've been to, which I still attend today. Most of my career has been about teaching and helping others become financially fit.

The principles in this book are not new, but I might have a different perspective on things or have a fresh way of describing things after sitting in front of my clients for almost 25 years. Hopefully the information in the book will jog your memory, help you learn new things and most importantly help you get the focus and motivation you need to move your finances forward. There are also some great stories from people who through their determination and hard work have become significantly better off — I'm sure you will enjoy reading them.

I absolutely believe that no matter your background or stage in life you can change your financial future if you make it important enough. I am extremely confident that you if you adopt the principles in this book you will become good with money and have a more financially free life.

STEP 1
Find your carrot

MONEY ISN'T EVERYTHING, but as the saying goes it ranks right up there with oxygen! Money is an essential part of our life; it doesn't necessarily make you happy — but having enough of it does go a long way towards making your life a lot easier, which may make you happier.

For some, money is a symbol of their success, but in my experience for most people money is purely a tool to help them put a roof over their head, look after their family, pay for life's necessities, and to have some fun and enjoy life. The challenge is often how much money you put towards living your life today as opposed to looking after your future self. It is not the easiest balancing act. Gaining clarity on what is important to you, setting some goals, and then charting a course to achieve those goals makes this balancing act a lot easier.

It's important to note that there isn't a magic formula for getting ahead financially. Many people I talk to or who come to me for advice want to know what the magic formula is or what the best investment tips are. Sorry to disappoint, but the 'magic' is as simple as spending less than you earn and investing the rest. If you do this for long enough, you will be financially independent. If getting ahead financially is simple, why are so many people challenged by it? Temptation! Life and stuff just get in the way. I didn't say it was easy, just simple.

How to find your carrot

In order to live your best life and one that you desire you must first find your carrot — your why, your dreams, your desires. *Finding your carrot* is the thing that helps you feel fired up or on a mission to make something a goal or priority. It's the thing that makes you want to wake up and jump out of bed in the morning. Your carrot is something that motivates you and will make you excited to achieve it. It's also something that, to you, is worth experiencing discomfort for!

All of us dream of success and wish to see our desires fulfilled. However, few of us achieve our dreams. This is because there is a big difference between wishing for something and having an intense, burning desire to achieve it. To live your best life, you first need to work out what it is and then you need to believe you deserve it and can achieve it — and then pursue it wholeheartedly. Choose your own path rather than that of others. Don't settle for what others think you should do. If you do that, finding the motivation and courage to pursue your goals will elude you.

The most difficult thing I find in helping people with their finances is getting them to actually do what they need to do. It's relatively straightforward for me to teach the technicalities of how to achieve financial freedom, as becoming financially free has little to do with investment expertise, although it certainly does help. Rather, it is about getting the basics right, doing them consistently over time and staying on track. Things like motivation, focus, hard work, patience, determination, desire, discipline and the like keep getting in the way! Many of us live our lives on the hamster wheel and never seem to have enough time to get things done. The more importance you place on your goals, and the clearer you are about what you want to achieve, the more likely you are to find the time to put the actions into place to succeed.

ELON MUSK is not your average human being. Zip2, PayPal, Tesla, SpaceX are just a few of the forward-thinking companies he's been behind. He taught himself how to code in three days; earned degrees in both physics and economics; borrowed books from friends and taught himself how to build rockets.

He is a billionaire several times over and has promised to send humans to Mars sometime before 2031. From anybody else this might seem a tad crazy. But coming from Musk, it sounds like something that just might be possible. He has an absolute unwavering belief and focus on his dreams.

Musk has a healthy scepticism for the status quo. Just because something has been done in a particular way for countless generations doesn't mean that it has to — or even should — stay that way. And just because you've lived your life in a particular way for seemingly countless years doesn't mean that you have to keep living it that way. You can change.

Musk said: 'I think people can choose to be not ordinary. They can choose to not necessarily conform to the conventions that were taught to them by their parents. Yes, I think it's possible to choose to be extraordinary.'

Elon Musk is without a doubt an exceptional individual. The reason I give him as an example is that he shows that even what many people think as the most unrealistic and craziest of goals, sending people to Mars, can be achieved. I fully believe that your dreams and goals can be achieved with the right focus, determination and action.

What is important to you

The next step in your journey to living your best life is to think about your priorities. Have you ever stopped to really think about which things are most important to you? Do you know how much time you spend on those priorities compared to less important things? Even if you are clear on your priorities, are you living in a way that is consistent with them right now?

Take a moment and imagine that you're at the end of your life and have a chance to give your current self some advice. What would you say? Many people find themselves saying things like 'spend more time on the things that really matter'. Here is a list of the common things people consider to be important in life:

- Family, spouse or partner
- Friends
- Health and fitness
- Where you live
- The amount of income you earn
- Your overall wealth and ability to save for the future
- How independent you are
- Making use of your talents with rewarding and stimulating work or hobbies
- Personal and professional growth
- How you can have a positive impact on society
- Security
- Spirituality or faith
- Having enough leisure and relaxation time
- Prestige and status

Find a quiet place where you can think, free from distractions. Write down what you consider is important, using the above list as a guideline. Rank your list, with the most important at the top based on your priorities at this point in your life (see below).

At the top of your list will be your **essentials** — the things that you consider most important and would hold on to at all costs. The next group are your **nice to haves** — things that are important to you but which you would be willing to let go of in certain situations. And the rest are your **non-essentials** — things that you would be willing to forgo. Choosing priorities is all about making trade-offs and deciding which things you're willing to compromise on in order to make the important stuff happen.

This can be a very difficult exercise as it forces you to realise that you can't have everything at any given point in your life — you will most likely have to make some difficult trade-offs.

Essentials

1. _____
2. _____
3. _____
4. _____
5. _____

Nice to haves

1. _____
2. _____
3. _____
4. _____
5. _____

Non-essentials

1. _____

2. _____

3. _____

4. _____

5. _____

The next step is to take an honest look at how you're living your life at the moment and decide whether this is consistent with your priority list. Take some time to redo the ranking exercise, but this time imagine that you've hired a detective who has been monitoring your activities 24 hours a day for the past few months. Now put your two lists side by side — how does the imaginary detective's ranking compare with your own priorities ranking? Are there any inconsistencies between how you would like to order your life and how you are living it? If so, consider how you might make changes in your life — at home, at work and beyond. What changes would it take to live in a way that really puts the important things first?

Here are some additional questions to consider:

What makes you happy and gets you excited?

_____

_____

What do you think and talk about most of the time: what do you want, or what don't you want?

_____

_____

Who do you love and want to be around you?

_____

_____

What do you want to achieve in your lifetime?

_____

_____

Where do you want to live and what type of lifestyle do you want?

_____

_____

What would your ideal day, week and year look like?

_____

_____

What are the activities that give you your greatest sense of meaning, fulfilment or purpose in life?

_____

_____

If the doctor said you had six months to live or you had unlimited money, what would you do differently?

_____

_____

Our priorities do change as we go through life, so it is good to check in again every few years. When facing a big life decision — such as a potential change in career, location or lifestyle — check in with your priority list. Will the change help you to live in a way that is closer to your real priorities, or will it take you further away from them?

DON'T WORRY ABOUT WHAT ANYONE ELSE THINKS

It is amazing how much energy we waste worrying about what others think. Bronnie Ware's 2012 book *The Top Five Regrets of the Dying* talks about living a life to minimise regrets. She spent many years in palliative care, looking after patients who had gone home to die. When she asked these patients about any regrets they had or anything they would do differently, a number of common answers were given.

The five most common themes were, in descending order:

1. I wish I'd had the courage to live a life true to myself, not the life others expected of me.
2. I wish I hadn't worked so hard.
3. I wish I'd had the courage to express my feelings.
4. I wish I'd stayed in touch with friends.
5. I wish that I'd let myself be happier.

The most common regret, by far, was 'I wish I'd had the courage to live a life true to myself, not the life others expected of me'. Too often, we don't focus on and spend enough time figuring out how we can live the happy life that we want. This leads to recriminations, self-doubt, blame and regrets. Create clarity around what and who is most important to you and your purpose, and then take the courageous steps to focus on only those things that truly matter. That way, you're far more likely to create a life well-lived, rather than one full of regrets.

Get your head in the right place

YOU ARE WHAT *YOU* BELIEVE

We create our own reality through what we think. The chances are that if you are confident you will succeed, you will. If you think you can't, you won't because you will focus on failure. Your external experiences always reflect your inner beliefs. If you heighten your belief in yourself, you can achieve greater things. So, to move forward in life you must change your beliefs.

Many of our beliefs and attitudes were developed when we were very young. We watch and learn from our parents, other family members, friends and teachers. Usually, we don't realise what we have picked up along the way and, unknowingly, we adopt their beliefs and experience as our own. While money management skills can be quite easily learnt, attitudes and behaviours are often more difficult to tackle. They can result from deeply ingrained beliefs or experiences. It's important that you realise what beliefs you have around money and establish which ones need to be changed.

Do any of these comments ring true for you?

- I don't earn enough.
- I don't deserve to have money.
- Money is the cause of all the world's problems; therefore, I never want to be wealthy.
- I'll never be good with money, so why even try.
- Managing money is hard.
- Money just seems to slip through my fingers.
- I am hopeless with money.
- Money doesn't grow on trees.
- I can only live my life fully if I have money.

- My friends seem to be doing well with money; something must be wrong with me.
- As long as I can pay my bills every month, I can spend the rest on having fun.
- Life is too short; I'll worry about retirement when I get older.
- Only going out with my friends and spending money is when we have fun.
- My friends wouldn't want to hang out with me if we did something for free.
- My parents never talked about money, so I guess I won't talk about it either.

Like it or not, money is one of the most important things in life. Everyone requires it and needs to know how to use it and manage it in their lives. Having a positive mindset is without a doubt the most important tool for becoming financially successful and being in control of your money. Most people think it's all about technical know-how, and then they come up with a range of excuses for why they aren't good with their money.

YOUR MONEY RELATIONSHIP

How healthy is your relationship with money? Numerous studies have shown that money is one of the leading causes of stress for adults, so having a healthy relationship with it will make a big difference to your financial success. What is your current relationship with money?

- You earn plenty of it but spend it faster than you earn it.
- You hold on tight to your money and agonise over spending any of it.
- You feel okay with the day-to-day stuff but are

overwhelmed by the bigger things, such as investing.
- You earn a low income and are sick and tired of struggling.
- You have no clue how much you actually owe, but it's probably a lot.
- You avoid opening any mail that looks like it might be a bill.
- You are always broke, and when you feel down you spend money you don't have.
- You make an okay income and seem to muddle through, but you don't really feel on top of things.
- You don't know how to organise your money and you feel out of control.
- You are always waiting anxiously for your next pay day.
- Your credit cards are always maxed to the limit.
- You are always borrowing money from friends or family.
- You feel embarrassed about the mess you feel you have made of your financial situation and are reluctant to seek help.

Do any of these statements sound like you? Do lots of them sound like you? Many people do not have a great relationship with money and have trouble managing it due to a whole range of reasons. Over the years I have worked with people from all walks of life, from low incomes to very high incomes, from different educational backgrounds, from different cultures, and their money issues tend to have a lot in common. For many people, being stressed about money or having money troubles often leads to low self-esteem and anxiety.

Describe your current relationship with money:

_____

_____

_____

_____

CREATE YOUR NEW REALITY

Influences — positive and negative — on your thoughts, attitudes and behaviours can come from anywhere. Partners, family, friends, work colleagues, the media, mentors and role models can affect what you believe and the choices you make. It's important to be able to identify where the different influences in your life are coming from and to make sure you absorb the positive but discard the negative. You don't necessarily need to ignore negative thoughts; rather, listen, see what you can learn and then move on. You can drown in them if you are not careful.

Does anyone you know laugh when you talk about starting a budget, tell you that you don't deserve something, tell you you're nuts when you talk about your dreams? I find it frustrating how often people are unsupportive and negative towards others.

Do you find it interesting that when you wake up and think you are going to have a bad day, you *actually* do? Imagine the situation: your alarm doesn't go off and you are now running late for work, you are hanging out for your regular morning coffee that you pick up on the way to work (which you seriously need today), but now it's cold and tastes lousy, and then there is an idiot driver in front of you. Or as my partner would say — they have no situational awareness! You are now at work and it seems as though everyone is giving you grief and everything is taking forever. You finally get home and tell yourself, 'I just knew it was going to be a lousy day — and it was!'

Now imagine this situation: you wake up before your alarm, feeling energised and excited about your day. There's time to have a leisurely shower, you pick up your morning coffee, the lady behind the counter smiles at you and your coffee tastes great. You arrive at work and your colleague says that you look nice today (possibly because you are radiating energy), you have a really productive day and come home saying to yourself what a great day it was. Quite a difference!

The effect of negativity in our lives is significant. Imagine a world where people constantly support and encourage each other: it would be incredible how much could be achieved. There are numerous research studies and books around this topic. If you feel this is an area of your life that needs more development, I would encourage you to seek out more information. A leader in this field is John Kehoe and I have personally read some of his books and attended his course.

Now that you have a clearer understanding of your beliefs around money and are aware how valuable it is to have a positive attitude, you will know if you need to change the way you look at money. Do you feel comfortable with your current beliefs, or do you need to develop some new and more positive ones? Some examples might be:

- I am in control of my money.
- What I don't know, I feel comfortable that I can learn.
- I know that being financially comfortable gives me more choices in my life.
- If I plan my week, I know that I will have time to manage my money.
- I know that managing my money is not that difficult — I just need to make a plan and stick to it, and take things one step at a time.
- I can achieve anything I put my mind to.
- I am really good at managing my money.
- I always spend my money wisely.
- I deserve happiness and success.
- I find it easy to manage my money.
- There is enough money for everyone.
- I always earn more than I spend.

Make a list of your new money beliefs:

_____

_____

_____

_____

Write down the way you would like your relationship with money to be:

_____

_____

_____

_____

Reprogram your mind with positive beliefs that will help you achieve your goals and throw away the negative beliefs that are holding you back. Positive beliefs work only if you truly believe in them. Remember that *you* are responsible for your beliefs about money — and you have the power to change these beliefs.

BOWL OVER THE BLOCKS

The next step in your journey is to get rid of the road blocks. Most of us will have some kind of fantasy about money lurking in our subconscious somewhere. Our brain can trick us into believing these fantasies could happen. If we really thought about it, it would become clear how silly they really are. Do any of the following sound familiar?

- *Lottery Living:* You believe you might nab a winning ticket . . . and you believe this every week.
- *I'm Gonna Marry a Millionaire:* And that single-minded

focus keeps you both single and broke. A man (or woman, for that matter) is not a financial plan.

- *Waiting for a Windfall:* Miscellaneous hopes for an inheritance, a bank error in your favour, a pot of gold in the back of the garage, etc.
- *Salary Hopes:* Thinking someone is going to pay you waaaaay more than they should, and you'll retire in two years.
- *Overnight Success:* You'll sell that screenplay or invent a new kind of peanut butter that will make you a gazillionaire.
- *Do What You Love, the Money Will Follow:* The title of an actual book that has created financial disaster for countless hopefuls.
- *Ignorance is Profitable:* The crackpot notion that by not paying attention to your money . . . one day you'll wake up rich!
- *Things Have a Way of Working Out:* When clearly they don't if you don't do anything about it.
- *I'll Do It Later:* Time has an uncanny ability of disappearing, and you wake up 30 years down the track still chanting to yourself that you have plenty of time and will do it later.
- *Money is Not Everything!* Try living without it for a month.
- *Denial:* I am not that out of shape.

Now at this point you are probably laughing. But I am sure that if you think about it, at some point at least one of these thoughts has gone through your head, or you have heard someone else say them. You might make these comments in jest — but what are you really thinking?

THE 'WHAT IFS' AND 'BUTS' DISEASE

So many people suffer from the 'what ifs' and 'buts' disease, otherwise known as *excusitis*. We can always find reasons why we shouldn't be doing something. That little chatterbox that sits inside our head is both very active and powerful. Be honest with yourself: are they good reasons or simply more excuses for you not to take action? Here are some of the common excuses I have come across over the years.

I wasn't taught in school, and my parents didn't teach me about money

Okay, most of us weren't taught about money when we were young. I think it's a real issue we have had with the curriculum in New Zealand. But that is the reality. It is well worth putting in the effort to improve your knowledge and there are lots of books, seminars, courses and experts out there that can help you learn about managing your money.

I'm too young to stress about saving money

When it comes to savings, age is never a factor. It is better to save money in the early stages of your career than regret not saving when an emergency arises. If you think that you can't enjoy your life without spending money, it may signify a deeper problem. Who says you can't have fun and save for a comfortable future simultaneously? You could gamify the activity to make it more fun by involving your friends.

I don't earn enough

The Millionaire Next Door, written by Tom Stanley and William Danko, sold millions of copies around the world, and it provides some fascinating insights into the average millionaire. Some of their findings were:

- They live in a fairly average house and over half have lived in the same house for more than 20 years.
- Their average taxable income was good but not as high as you might think.
- For the most part, millionaires describe themselves as 'tightwads' and don't spend a lot of money.
- Most drive older cars and only a minority drive new cars or lease vehicles.
- They are dedicated investors and on average invest nearly 20% of their income every year.

Getting ahead financially is not about how much you earn; it's about where you spend your money and living within your means.

It's my job to look after the kids; my partner handles the finances

Love is what makes our life special, but without money it can be quite difficult. We have a growing single population, people are getting married later, divorce rates are high, and one partner often outlives the other. There is a fairly good chance that you will be alone for some part of your adult life. If your partner is good with money and you aren't, you may be happy for them to take day-to-day responsibility for your finances — but at the very least, you need to be aware of what they are doing.

I don't understand these things; I don't have the brains to understand

Talent is overrated. Dr Benjamin Bloom of the University of Chicago conducted a five-year study of leading artists, athletes and scholars. It consisted of anonymous interviews with the top 20 performers in various fields, including pianists, Olympic swimmers, tennis players, sculptors, mathematicians and neurologists. That information was supplemented by additional interviews with those people's families and teachers. Bloom and his team of researchers sought to find clues to how these high achievers developed. What they discovered was that drive and determination — not talent — led to their success. I totally believe that everyone, given some effort on their part, has the ability to understand basic money principles. You do not have to be a financial wizard to be a good money manager.

I don't have enough time; there are never enough hours in the day

Time management is a common problem. Most people today are time-poor. Have a look at your day:

- How do you spend it?
- What ruts have you slipped into that you could easily free yourself from?
- What poor habits are eating valuable minutes of your life every day?
- Constantly ask yourself, 'Is what I am doing now a good use of my time?'
- What impact can a few minutes make? Take a look at this. What if you were able to save . . .

  5 minutes by streamlining your morning routine (taking less time to dress, shave, put on make-up, drink coffee, read the paper and so on)?

  10 minutes by eliminating the things you do each morning to stall starting your workday?

  5 minutes by avoiding idle talkers or other distractions?

  10 minutes by taking a shorter lunch or break time?

Now those minutes don't seem like much. But if you did those things every day, five days a week, for 50 weeks, you would gain an additional 125 hours of time every year. That's equivalent to about three 40-hour weeks to use for anything you want!

I am overwhelmed by too much information

Information certainly is growing exponentially. Today, in a weekend paper from any large city there is more information than the majority of the people living in the 1700s would have access to in an entire lifetime. Most of us today feel as though we are drowning in data. We may not be able to change the volume of information, but we can control the way we handle it.

I want to wait until . . . my next pay rise/next year/the kids go to school, etc.

As I mentioned earlier, we can always find some excuse for procrastinating. The problem is that we often keep finding excuses to the point where it gets put off forever. Ask yourself honestly if it is just another excuse or if it is a good reason.

I don't have the energy it takes

The potential energy we have in all of us is enormous. How many times have you done something that you procrastinated over for ages and then after you did it you said to yourself, 'It didn't take as long as I thought' or 'That wasn't as bad as I thought'? In the words of Thomas Edison, 'If we did all the things we are capable of, we could literally astound ourselves.'

I am afraid of making a mistake and failing

Obviously if you never try to do something, you will never fail. But then you aren't likely to succeed, either. Success doesn't miraculously appear out of the blue. It's always the result of a concrete action and a positive mental attitude. Everyone fails at times; it is just part of life. The important thing is to learn from your failures and mistakes so that you eventually become successful.

You may have thousands of excuses but no good reasons.

YOU CAN ABSOLUTELY CHANGE YOUR THINKING

You read earlier how negative emotions are the enemies of success. They can consume you, zap your energy and take away your happiness. You need to learn how to remove negative emotions from your life. How many times have you dreaded doing something because it was going to be difficult? You put it off and put it off, procrastinating for weeks on end . . . then finally you get around to doing it. You have spent so much time believing it was going to be difficult that, even when you've performed the task and found that it was pretty easy after all, you still believe it was difficult because you talked yourself into believing it so.

Ridding yourself of negative emotions is an integral part of your success in taking control of your life. Observe your emotions and thoughts over the coming weeks. Are they positive or negative? Just being aware of them helps you begin to create change.

- Stop justifying things.
- Stop rationalising and making excuses for your behaviour.
- Don't worry about what other people think; what's

important is what *you* think.

- Realise that you alone are responsible for your thoughts and behaviours.
- Stop blaming others.
- Be more aware of your emotions.
- Don't sweat the small stuff.

Resolve today that you will no longer dwell on these myths, fantasies and excuses. Decide to adopt more positive emotions and thoughts about money in the future.

Establish your starting point

Now that you have spent some time considering what *you* want your ideal life to look like, what is important to you and getting your head in the right place by removing any blocks, the next step is to start putting a plan in place to control your finances effectively and build your financial future. The first thing you need to do is establish your starting point by working out your **net worth.** A Net Worth Statement is a snapshot of your current financial situation and will give you important clues about where you should concentrate your efforts.

Imagine you are going on a diet; many of us can relate to this. The first thing you need to do is weigh yourself so you know what your current weight is. Then you can form a plan to get to the weight you want to be. Managing your finances is very similar. And just as maintaining a good weight depends on good eating and exercise habits, being successful financially depends on good money habits.

Your net worth is the difference between all the things of value that you **own**, and all the debts you **owe**. In financial terms, your net worth is your assets minus your liabilities.

Effectively if you sold everything today how much money would you have in your hand? Calculating your net worth is fairly simple to do.

Draw up a table and put all of your assets in one column and list their value, and all the liabilities in the other column. Note that you don't want to include things like clothing and furniture as they really don't have much value. Also, many people include their life insurance policy (unless it is a policy that has an investment component); don't include this as it's only of use to your beneficiaries, not you. When allocating values, be conservative. It's best to underestimate than overestimate. Let's look at an example:

NET WORTH STATEMENT (EXAMPLE)

Assets	Value	Liabilities	Value
Home	$800,000	Home mortgage	$400,000
KiwiSaver	$120,000	Credit cards	$10,000
Cash in bank	$20,000	Consumer debt	
Shares	$2,000	Car loan	$15,000
Superannuation		Loan from family	
Property investments		Investment/business debt	
Business			
Total Assets	$942,000	Total Liabilities	$425,000
Total Net Worth (Assets — Liabilities) = $517,000			

Is the number positive (the value of the assets is greater than the liabilities)? If it is, you have a positive net worth. This is a good thing. If the number is negative (more liabilities than assets), you have a negative net worth. Of course, this is not such a good thing. Regardless of where you are starting your financial journey from, the most important thing is that you have the information.

Now you know what your starting point is, and you have a reference point from which to track your financial progress. It's a good idea to track this every year so you know how things are going. It's also a great motivation tool when you see your net worth increasing over time. Interestingly, for many of my clients, this exercise really seems to help get them motivated.

The median net worth of New Zealand households for the year ended June 2021 was $397,000; up 21% from $328,000 for the year ended June 2018. The increase in net worth was largely driven by an increase in the value of owner-occupied dwellings, other real estate, and property held in family trusts. Property values are based on the capital (rateable) value at the time of the survey.

Individual net worth typically increases with age until retirement. Young people (15–24 years) had the lowest median individual net worth ($3,000), while people in the traditional retirement ages (65–74 years) had the highest ($433,000).

Source: NZ Stats — Household net worth statistics: Year ended June 2021

Chart your course

The next step in your journey is to aim your efforts in the right direction and set some goals. One of the great benefits of goal-setting is that it enables you to control the direction of your life. Your goals may be more like dreams or long-term visions, but they're a good starting point. When you have a strong desire to achieve your dreams it helps you find the energy and the internal drive to overcome all the obstacles that will arise along your journey. But they do need to be put into some kind of plan. Research shows that people who set, work towards and achieve goals are vastly more successful than those who don't.

Harvard University conducted a study between 1979 and 1989. At the outset, the graduates of the MBA programme were asked, 'Have you set clear, written goals for your future and made plans to accomplish them?' It turned out that only 3% of the graduates had written goals and plans. Thirteen per cent had goals, but they weren't in writing. Eighty-four per cent had no goals other than finishing their course and enjoying the summer.

Ten years later, the researchers interviewed the members of that class again. They found that the 13% who had had unwritten goals were earning on average twice as much as the 84% who had no goals. But most surprisingly, they found that the 3% of graduates who had clear, written goals when they left Harvard were earning, on average, 10 times as much as the other 97%. The only difference between the groups was the clarity of the goals they had for themselves when they graduated.

There are lots of ways to plan to achieve your goals. The best strategy I've found is to broadly outline your short, medium and long term goals, then break them down into a more specific annual plan, and then into monthly or weekly tasks.

One of the most well-known approaches for effective goal-setting is the **SMART System** — **S**pecific, **M**easurable, **A**chievable, **R**ealistic and with a **T**ime frame. Each time you write down a goal consider the following:

- **Specific** — Is the goal specific?
- **Measurable** — Are you able to measure it?
- **Achievable** — Do you think this goal is achievable if you are focused, committed and prepared to put in the effort?
- **Realistic** — If you are honest with yourself, is your goal realistic for you to achieve?

- Time frame — A task will always expand to fill the number of hours you devote to it, so allocate a time frame.

Always write down your goals and put them in a place where you regularly see them. I don't believe having goals only in your head will work. Use the examples below as a guide:

Work (work towards a promotion; increase business turnover by 15% this financial year)

Short term: _____

Medium term: _____

Long term: _____

Personal (*do a university paper; invite friends around for dinner one night every month*)

Short term: _____

Medium term: _____

Long term: _____

Health (*learn to play tennis, lose 5 kg*)

Short term: _____

Medium term: _____

Long term: _____

Family/Relationships (*take partner/family away for a two-week holiday*)

Short term: _____

Medium term: _____

Long term: _____

Financial (*complete budget every month, increase mortgage payments, pay off credit card, create an investment plan, increase your financial knowledge, save for a house deposit*)

Short term: _____

Medium term: _____

Long term: _____

DEVELOP YOUR PERSONAL ANNUAL PLANNER

Now that you have your list of goals and know if they are short, medium or long term, you need to break them down into an annual planner or task list. As you are doing this, ask yourself these questions:

- Are your short-term goals in line with your long-term ones?
- Do your short-term goals take you closer to achieving your long-term goals?
- Are they **SMART** goals?

DEVELOP YOUR TASK LIST

Now that you have established your goals and worked out which ones you want to achieve this year, break them down into monthly or weekly manageable tasks. Don't worry too much about the time frame but rather decide which is most effective for you.

I had a client once who was really tired of his life, wasn't in a good financial position after his divorce and wanted to make changes. He worked out his quarterly rather than annual goals, broke them down into monthly ones and then daily. Every day he started with what he wanted to achieve that day and was incredibly focused. And, boy, did he get some amazing results.

Below is an example of a task list. It is designed so that it is simple to use, easy to complete and ideal to put on the fridge or somewhere you see regularly. Again, just find a method that works for you.

No.	Task	By whom	Due date	Completed
1	Carry a notebook to track spending for a month	Mary Tom	1 month	
2				
3				
4				
5				
6				
7				

REVIEW YOUR PROGRESS

I cannot stress enough how important it is to regularly review your progress. I think it is most effective to do this weekly, especially when you are starting out, or you might do what my client did and review them daily. You may find that after a while you can reduce the frequency; however, anything longer than a month and you may find yourself falling off the wagon. It can be helpful to check in with a friend or partner.

Review questions

Here are some questions you can ask yourself, or have your partner/friend ask you, each time you do your review. They may help keep you focused.

What are the top two thoughts that have limited my progress?

_____

_____

_____

What are the top two things I am going to stop doing?

_____

_____

_____

What are the top two things I am going to start doing?

_____

_____

_____

What did I learn?

_____

_____

_____

How can I be more effective?

_____

_____

_____

What did I accomplish? What are the top two things that I did well?

_____

_____

_____

On a scale of 0–10 what was my commitment level this week? What do I want it to be next week?

This week _____ Next week_____

'A journey of a thousand miles begins with a single step.'
–CONFUCIUS

TIPS FOR STAYING ON TRACK

- Realise you will not achieve a goal or aspiration until that goal becomes a priority. Remember it takes a good 21 days to establish a new habit.
- Set aside a regular time for your review; picking the same time each week or month will likely help.
- Make yourself accountable for your goals.
- Don't beat yourself up or criticise your partner if you don't achieve all your goals; instead, resolve to do better next week.
- Pat yourself on the back if you achieve what you set out to do.
- Create an agenda for your review and stick to it. It's amazing what you can achieve in a short time if you are focused.

- Don't spend too much time during your week thinking about how well you are doing; save it for your review time. You can waste a lot of time going around in circles and over-analysing.
- If you are in a relationship, share the tasks according to where your strengths lie, and be sure to support and encourage each other.
- Remember: one small step at a time.

When first starting this review process, you may find that it takes more time than you would like. It takes practice to get it right.

JUST DO IT!

The primary difference between high achievers and low achievers is *action orientation*. Those who accomplish a lot in their lives are very action oriented. They are always busy, always moving, and when they have an idea they immediately take action on it. Remember: these actions don't need to be huge tasks. It is not necessarily the size of the steps or actions you take, it's the amount and the consistency. For example, before you buy anything ask yourself if you really need it, instead of just splashing out. Pausing to think will take only a moment, and if you do it often enough you will create a good money habit that could save you thousands in the long run. Resolve today to begin taking those small steps each day towards achieving your goals.

SUCCESS
Select your goal
Unlock your personal potential
Commit yourself to your plan
Chart your course
Expect problems
Stand firm on your commitment
Start today

Case Study: Achieving financial freedom (Bradie — Te Awamutu)

My earliest memory of money management was when I was around eight years old. I received fortnightly pocket money under my pillow, which I learnt to budget by reading my father's budget book. It was the start of my love of budgeting.

At the tender age of 13, I walked the main street of my local town, visiting each bank and branch, asking for their best savings rates. At 16, I fully funded a return trip to Sydney with my girlfriend. At the time, I worked in a part-time job every day after school, at weekends and during holidays. My first full-time job was working as a cash-teller for a local bank. It was a dream come true to be able to work with money all day!

I got married at 20 and we had our three children not long after. Our finances weren't a priority at this time. We were living pay cheque to pay cheque and trying to make ends meet, as well as working on climbing the property ladder. We tried our hand at property investing, but it wasn't for us and by 45, I was so sick and tired of having no money and robbing Peter to pay Paul that I knew something had to change.

I was about to receive three big wake-up calls that would change my life forever.

The first monumental moment in my life happened in December 2015 when I lost my eldest sister to cancer. She had been such a huge influence on me and a major part of my life that I felt like I had literally lost an arm when she passed away. I was lucky enough to spend the last four weeks of her life by her side, and one thing she taught me was to be happy, and that you have to 'stand in your truth'. I didn't realise it at the time, but I wasn't anywhere near to standing in mine.

The next moment was a weekend in January 2016, when my husband and I went to stay with some friends in Taranaki. While there, my friend and I decided to go and do a spot of shopping. We went to a lovely homewares store and I saw and fell in love with a canvas of a 'Buddha'. It was one of my sister's favourite things and I just knew I had to have it. I bought it with our credit card as we didn't have any spare money in our account. When I got home with my purchase, my husband was shocked. He asked, 'How did you pay for it?' and I said it was on the card. He was less than pleased (to say the least) and our trip home was mostly silent. At the time, I didn't understand what the big deal was, as it was only a few hundred dollars. Little did I know I was soon to find out.

The final moment was another weekend away in January 2016 with my sister and brother-in-law to Auckland. We were out for dinner at the Food Truck (using the credit card, of course) and decided to go to the the movies. We found out that *The Big Short* was playing just down the road, so with ice creams in hand, we ran and arrived in the nick of time.

If you don't know it, this movie is set in the USA during the Financial Crisis of 2007–08. The banks were calling up loans all over the place and people were losing their homes. I went home after this movie and my husband and I, along with my sister and brother-in-law, were up until 1 am discussing finances. It dawned on me that we were not paying $1 towards reducing the debt we owed. All of our loans were 'interest only'. My home has always been my 'safe place', but at that moment, I realised it wasn't really safe. The bank owned it, and if we missed our payments, we could lose our home. The next morning, on 16 January 2016, we decided enough was enough; it was time for me to stand in my truth, get real, and start paying off our debt. I googled 'how to become debt free' and US financial personality Dave Ramsey came up. We started following his baby steps to financial freedom.

Once we arrived home, and the kids were in bed, we sat down for our first budget meeting together. This was one of the lowest points of my life. My husband was always good with money and had been saving all his pocket money for a rainy day. He had around $800 saved in his wallet. I was the opposite and didn't have a penny to my name. What's more, I had incurred credit card debt of $3,500 on 'stuff' I couldn't explain. We added up all our debt and it came to a staggering $566,000. I was in disbelief and shock and felt I was to blame as I was always in charge of the finances.

Over the next 39 months, we turned our financial situation around. We started off by saving $1,000 as an emergency fund. We had never had any savings before, so this felt amazing. We opened a separate savings account so the emergency fund money couldn't be touched and went on to the next step.

Credit cards had always been our emergency fund. I often used them if we had no money left in our account. We cut them up and cancelled them. We had over $3,500 of debt on them and interest was accruing at a horrific rate. We wanted immediate action, so I came up with an idea to downsize our car. I was driving a Holden Captiva for my five-minute trip to work, so we decided to sell it and buy something smaller and more economical. We sold the Holden for $15,000 and bought a Toyota for $9,000. With the difference we paid off the credit cards and topped up our emergency fund to $4,000. We had finally started to get some traction.

Since we had sold the car and did well, we thought, gosh, what else can we sell? We had a whole lot of stuff in our house, so, man, did we go hard. Anything that wasn't tied down was sold. The more the better. We made another $2,000 which went straight into the emergency fund. We kept saving for a few more months until finally we had established a fund of $10,000. I couldn't have been prouder and I slept so much better at night knowing that our lifestyle was fully funded.

During this process, I kept refining our budget. Each month I found ways to trim our expenses. I treated it as my 'second job' and cut back on everything. Our Sky subscription went, insurances were cut. Groceries became like a full-time job: writing a list, checking specials, meticulously planning our weekly menus. I even ventured into making our own soap and washing machine powder. It was fun living the simple life and we were in our element. The more money we saved, the more it spurred us on.

Once we had our emergency fund in place and our monthly expenses down to $2,000, we decided we were ready to deal to our mortgages. We had $563,000 on two loans. We sold our rental property for $315,000 and so had $248,000 of mortgage debt left. It was on a fixed rate, but I was able to increase the payments. I raised the amount to my entire pay cheque. Man, was that scary! It was $1,848 a fortnight and we were living on my husband's pay. He was working six days a week and taking every extra shift that he could. He was incredible during this time, and probably at his happiest as I wasn't spending!

We had a few obstacles to overcome during the time we were paying off our mortgage. We were in a self-imposed lockdown so things weren't easy. We had to say 'no' a lot to our friends and family who were going out and doing things. At first it was hard, but then they stopped asking. We also got push-back from the bank when we wanted to make extra payments of $10,000 off our mortgage. At one point, the bank assistant told me to put the funds on term deposit until such time as our mortgage came off fixed. I didn't take 'no' for an answer, and kept asking, until finally the area manager agreed that I could make a 'partial break'. We did this every time we saved another $10,000 (this took us around six months at a time). We also had a break-in during this time, had to pay for security, had emergency dentist visits, a family member had a car crash — so we had to dig very deep at times.

A lot of wonderful things also happened along the way. Two granddaughters arrived at this time, and we had a lovely simple holiday in Noosa visiting friends. I shared my story on Instagram and gained over 15,000 followers. I did guest appearances on a few podcasts and appeared in newspapers and on TV and got so much lovely feedback.

Paying off our mortgage took us a total of 39 months. It took blood, sweat and tears, but on 17 April 2019 we were officially debt free. We were aged 48 and 55. One of the best days of my life.

Next step — investing! If I loved paying off debt, investing is a whole different level of enjoyment. I started off dabbling in buying shares through platforms like Sharesies and Smartshares. I also read every book I could get my hands on about investing. Now I follow a few key people on Instagram and get their daily updates. I listen to financial podcasts on investing and soak up every bit of information that I can. We try to invest up to 50% of our income, but we don't always achieve this.

We always had 'downsizing' as a prospect in our future and realised we had a lot of capital secured in our family home. As our children had now all flown the nest and we had a large home and section, we decided it was time for a change. We first looked around our town and eventually found a builder who would offer a fixed-price contract so we could get our house ready for the market. We worked hard on this step and did everything we could to get our home in its best shape ever. It was sparkling inside and out. We were very lucky to time the market and we sold our property at the peak in 2021/22. We managed to free up a substantial amount of capital that we could invest for our retirement.

Our next step is to keep investing, until we reach our targeted retirement amount. We have worked out a set amount that we think will provide us with a comfortable retirement with a few luxuries. I'm not sure that we will ever 'retire' but instead may be 'work optional'. I would like to write my own book one day, finish my finance papers and help others to get ahead in their financial life. That is my true calling.

I would like to end with a quote from Ellen Goodman:

'Normal is getting dressed in clothes that you buy for work, driving through traffic in a car that you are still paying for, in order to get to a job that you need so you can pay for the clothes, car and the house that you leave empty all day in order to afford to live in it.'

In a Nutshell
- Knowing what is important to you gives you focus and motivation.
- It only matters what *you* think — not what anyone else does.
- Develop a positive and purposeful relationship with money.
- Successful people always set goals — set yours.
- Become action oriented, as it is the difference between low achievers and high achievers.

STEP 2

Develop your money system

There are only two things you can do with money: save it or spend it. If you spend it, it's gone forever!

NOW YOU HAVE GOT your head in the right place and set some goals, the next thing in building your financial foundations is creating a solid money system. This is possibly one of the most important things you can do for your financial health. Unfortunately, for many people it is also one of the toughest. Why? It often means you must make choices that you don't wish to make.

You only get to spend each of your hard-earned dollars once, so you want to make sure that you spend them as wisely as possible. Consider the following:

- Are you making conscious decisions about where you spend your money or are your decisions being made subconsciously through the habits that you have? In other words, are you making proactive financial decisions or are you scratching your head at the end of each month wondering where your money went?
- Are you spending your money on things that are really important and valuable to you or on stuff that doesn't mean a lot?
- Are you spending your money on things that boost your ego but deflate your wealth? They make you feel good today, but they have a future cost which may be a higher price than you are willing to pay.

1. The notebook exercise

One of the best things to do to help you create your money system is the notebook exercise. It is probably the most annoying exercise you will ever do when trying to manage your money better and yet it is also one of the most effective. In my experience many people are not entirely sure what they spend their money on, and many have no idea at all. The notebook exercise lets you work out exactly where your money goes each month. Before developing a realistic money management system, you need to understand exactly where your money is going — and I mean *exactly*.

We live in a society where material things are generally considered important and where spending is encouraged, whether or not we have the money. We are constantly being exposed to businesses advertising their products and enticing us to buy. Our discretionary spending (our wants), rather than our needs, is where our money often disappears, without us really being aware of where it goes.

SO WHERE TO START?

Buy a small notebook (a piece of paper divided into 30 sections will also work). You can also use the notepad on your smartphone. For one month keep a record of *every dollar* you spend and what you spend it on. Don't forget to write down the price of your notebook. If you are moaning and groaning right now, suck it up. It's only for one month — you will cope! I have yet to come across anyone who wasn't surprised to learn how much money they spent on things that they had no idea about.

It is useful to write down everything, including things like rent or mortgage payments, petrol, food and utilities. While it's difficult to change how much you spend on necessities, it is still important to know as these figures will be used in creating your money system. However, people are surprised how much typically discretionary items can add up to, such as meals out, takeaways, Uber Eats, magazines, chocolate bars, clothes and the like. Technology has made it harder to keep track in many ways because payments automatically come out of your bank account or are put on credit. You don't have the same awareness you would if you used cash, which in today's world is often surprisingly difficult to use.

Be totally honest with yourself — otherwise there's no point in going through this exercise. The information you gather will be very helpful in the next exercises to build your money system. It's best to make a note of your expenditure at the time you spend it or at the very least each day. Otherwise, it's too easy to forget.

Your list will be varied, and on top of your necessities it may include things like:

- lunches, snacks (you can take your lunch which is cheaper)
- coffees and drinks

- cigarettes
- takeaways or Uber Eats
- magazines
- online subscriptions
- sweets
- clothes and make-up
- Lotto tickets
- books
- knick-knacks
- flowers
- kids' toys
- entertainment

This may seem a tedious exercise. Stay with it, though, as it can be very empowering to learn how money slips through your fingers.

A while back I provided the financial advice behind the popular New Zealand TV show *Money Man* for four years. One of the key things we did to steer people back on track financially was to get them to carry a notebook around with them for a month. They all swore they had absolutely no spare money. Interestingly, they all discovered that they spent a lot more than they thought they did. Most of the candidates on the show, especially in the first season, earned only the average wage, if that. Most were based in Auckland and were earning $30,000 to $50,000 as an individual or around $50,000 to $70,000 as a household.

Their average monthly spend on miscellaneous discretionary stuff that had little value was between $400 and $700. Given that was about 15 years ago, those numbers in a similar situation today could be double. That's a lot of money slipping through your fingers when you don't earn a lot. This was one of the key areas where we were able to help people make changes so they

The Notebook Method

Day 1.	Day 2.	Day 3.
Day 4.	Day 5.	Day 6.
Day 7.	Day 8.	Day 9.
Day 10.	Day 11.	Day 12.
Day 13.	Day 14.	Day 15.
Day 16.	Day 17.	Day 18.
Day 19.	Day 20.	Day 21.
Day 22.	Day 23.	Day 24.
Day 25	Day 26.	Day 27.
Day 28.	Day 29.	Day 30.

could put that money towards things that were more valuable, such as repaying debt or building up savings.

At the other end of the income scale, one of my clients who was earning $7,000 per month in the hand (after tax) did the same exercise. When she came to see me, she had completed her income-and-expenditure form, which indicated that she was spending around $3,000 per month. So, of course, I asked where the bank account was into which she was putting the extra $4,000 from her earnings. Not surprisingly, there was no bank account — she was spending the entire $7,000.

It is not uncommon for high-income earners to spend like this, and I'm not saying it's wrong. But if you want to get ahead financially, you need to make good decisions on how you spend your money. When we redid her budget we put some of that $4,000 into her budget for spending, some into reducing her mortgage and $1,500 into an investment plan. That was about 10 years ago and today she is in a much stronger financial position, which has enabled her to have more choices in her life. She is very glad she went through the exercise and made some changes.

The key purpose of this exercise is to give you more information, which will enable you to make better choices with your money. It's not about stopping all your discretionary spending and making major sacrifices. It is about having more awareness and making decisions that serve you better.

2. Rank your spending

After doing the notebook exercise, the reality is that most of you will need to cut back on some of your spending to make your money system work. Spending more than you earn is something far too many people do, and it is not a great recipe for financial success. Ideally you want to find a balance with your spending, so that you can put some money aside but, at the same time, not feel as though you are making too many sacrifices.

If you are in a lot of debt, you may need to make more sacrifices until you get ahead and your debt is paid off (see Chapter 4 on dealing with debt). As I explained with the notebook exercise, there may well be things you are buying that you do not really need.

LOW-SACRIFICE VERSUS HIGH-SACRIFICE SPENDING

The next step in preparing to develop your money system is to rank your discretionary spending from high sacrifice to low sacrifice. High-sacrifice items are those of high importance to you and which you would really miss if you went without them. Low-sacrifice items are those that you have fallen into the habit of buying but probably would not miss a lot if you didn't have them, or you could easily find an alternative.

If you've been filling out the notebook with your expenditures, you don't have to wait until the end of the month to start this next exercise. If you start after, say, a week of beginning your notebook, you may want to check in at the end of the month to ensure you haven't missed anything. Any items that count as essential spending will need to go into your money system.

In this exercise we are concerned with the discretionary items — your wants — the ones that you don't have to have but you would like to have. Alongside each item on your list put a ranking from 1 to 10, 1 indicating low sacrifice (you wouldn't miss them) and 10 being high sacrifice (it'd be very hard to go without them).

I came across this concept in a health book that explained how to design a sustainable eating plan. For me, chocolate is a high-sacrifice food, as I really like it and would probably develop a craving for it and start dreaming of giant-sized chocolate bars if I didn't occasionally have some! Potatoes or bread would be my low-sacrifice foods. As for spending, a high-sacrifice item would be my gym membership and a low sacrifice would be a magazine.

To create your money system, you need to decide which items you want to keep. They will be the ones that are the most important to you and will be close to 10 in your ranking. Once you have done this, ensure they make financial sense and will fit into your money system and are aligned with your financial goals. If your monthly sanity money is $200, which items can you buy (and how often)? You will probably need to cut down on both the number of different items and the frequency. Getting the mix right for your situation may take some tweaking.

The items that don't make the final list are maybe things that you buy only occasionally when you have some extra money. It doesn't matter what is on your final list, as long as it fits into your plan. There will also be some items that you can find alternatives to, such as:

- Magazines — you could get them from the library, or just buy fewer, swap with friends, get the same information online.
- Takeaways or lunches — rather than have them, say, two or three times per week, buy them once a week or once a month. Use one of the meal delivery companies like My Food Bag. They may seem a little expensive on the surface, but I'm sure they will be cheaper than takeaways. It also may reduce your food wastage and is probably a lot healthier. Some of my clients buy a food bag for more people than are in their household and use the leftovers for lunch the next day.

- Clothing — you will be amazed at what you can buy second hand. I know some people have a stigma about this, but think about how much you could save and put towards something that is really valuable to you.
- Children's toys — you could swap with friends or use the toy libraries that are all around the country. You can get new toys on a regular basis and there is a bonus of less plastic that goes into the environment.

	Item	Ranking
1.		
2.		
3.		
4.		
5.		
6.		
7.		
8.		
9.		
10.		
11.		
12.		
13.		
14.		
15.		
16.		
17.		
18.		
19.		
20.		

> **Did you know?** The average millionaire spends one minute longer thinking about their buying decision than the average person. Do they really want it, do they really need it, can they get better value using their money for something else?

3. Create your money system

Now you are on to the exciting stuff — well, at least I think it is exciting — and the next step is to create your money system. What is a money system? It's my name for a budget. I like this term because the word 'budget' has so many negative connotations and many people seem to switch off as soon as they hear it. They think of things like hard, tough, sacrifice, difficult, challenging . . . Admittedly, managing your money can be hard at times, especially at the beginning. However, it can also be liberating, freeing, uplifting and empowering. A successful money system enables you to make better decisions about your money. There are so many benefits to having one.

You can call your money system whatever you want. Another term I often use is 'spending plan'. Find a word or phrase that has a positive feeling for you. There is no right or wrong way to manage your money; it just needs to work for you and be reasonably easy for you to manage once it's set up. Try to keep it fairly simple because if you make it too complicated and overthink it, it can become too hard, and you will be more likely to give up. It needs to become a habit: something that you don't have to think too much about because it happens automatically.

I often get asked what the best budgeting system is. I do not believe there is one. No 'one size fits all'. The most important thing is to create a system that you feel will work for your individual circumstances and that you can sustain. Below are some examples of the system that I think is the most effective and have used with my clients for many years. There are three types:

- **Personal money system** — this is ideal for people who are on wages or salaries
- **Business money system** — this is an expanded version for those who have a business
- **Total money system** — which takes into account both the above and adds in long-term savings

YOUR PERSONAL MONEY SYSTEM

First up is your personal money system which is the basis for all systems. Let's explore the type of accounts you might use.

Day-to-day account

This is where you would pay for all the monthly essentials, such as rent/mortgage, groceries, insurance, school fees, repayments, petrol, car maintenance, telephone, electricity and the like. Essentially, all the things that you have to have.

Big-ticket account or special purpose

This is where you save up for those bigger costs — things that you would like to have but don't necessarily need (holidays, upgrading the car, home renovations, furniture, etc.).

Rainy-day account

A rainy-day or emergency account for when something happens that you hadn't planned on. It is always best in a separate account. It's useful to have this account in case you get large, unexpected bills, or if you are off work. It means you don't need to pay the bills with your credit card, borrow money from other sources or face the stress that comes with these unplanned expenses. You want at least three months, or in an ideal world six months, of your expenses or living costs tucked away. Having this account limits you getting derailed when you get a bill you didn't expect and helps with your peace of mind as you know you have money set aside.

Debt-reduction or savings account

This is where you should put as much money as you can afford. If you have debts, this is where you can set aside any extra money you have to pay them off quicker. Once they are gone you can start to build up your savings. Or if you don't have any debt, you can start saving straight away — maybe towards a house deposit; if you already have a home, you could make extra mortgage payments or start a long-term savings and investment plan.

Sanity money

Otherwise known as pocket money, this is what you can use to buy discretionary items (wants). Some of my clients call it their fun account. It is here that people typically spend a lot more than they think they do. Often the best way to manage your sanity money is to take it out of the ATM in cash once a week, fortnight or month, depending on how you manage your budget. The important thing with sanity money is that you don't spend any more than your allowance.

PERSONAL MONEY SYSTEM (EXAMPLES)

Example 1

Jason earns $60,000 per year or $5,000 per month after tax. He has accumulated a lot of personal debts. He has worked out that he needs $3,000 per month to pay his rent, groceries, petrol and all bills. Getting out of debt so he can start saving for a house deposit is really important to him so he has decided to focus on this as a priority. He will give himself $200 of sanity money each month, $500 will go into his rainy-day account and the balance of $1,300 will go towards paying off his debts. Once he has $9,000 in his rainy-day account (equivalent to three months of his expenses) he will put the $500 into additional debt repayments.

Jason salary

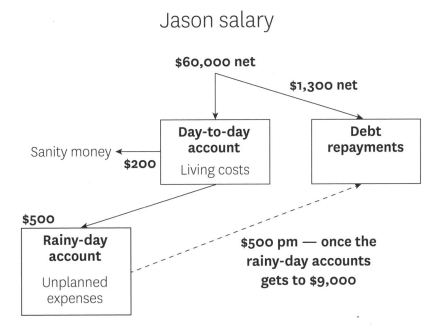

Example 2

Ben and Jenny earn annual salaries of $70,000 and $50,000 net (after tax is taken out) respectively, or $10,000 per month in total. Both of their incomes go into their day-to-day bank account. They have worked out that they need $7,000 to pay bills and the minimum on their mortgage each month, which leaves $3,000 for them to decide what to do with. They chose to give themselves $250 cash per month each for spending money, $500 into their rainy-day account (note once the value gets to three to six months of your monthly expenses you could add this to one of your other accounts), $500 into their big-ticket account, $500 into a holiday account (they decided they preferred to separate this out) and then add an extra $1,000 payment to their mortgage so it could be paid off faster.

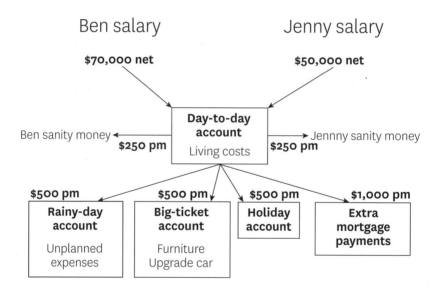

Example 3

Here is another option for Ben and Jenny where they live on Ben's income and put all of Jenny's salary towards paying off the mortgage. Their minimum mortgage payments are $3,000 per month or $36,000 per year so they are paying an additional $14,000 per year off their mortgage, which will mean they pay off their mortgage a lot faster and save a lot in interest (see page 156 for some examples).

This is not necessarily a better option, just a different one that may suit them better.

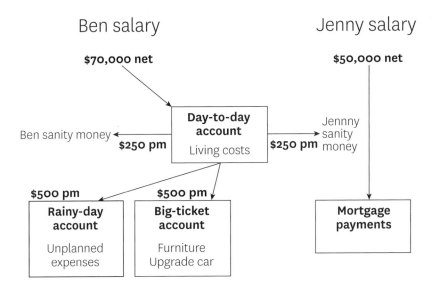

The above option is a good one to consider when planning for a baby. Live off the income you are going to keep and then put the other income into a savings account so you have money during your maternity period. Or if you want to live on one income long term, you will have time to practise and see how having just the one income could work for you.

The above illustrations are examples only. Create your own system that you think will suit your situation. I have found this type of system to be the most effective. Once you have an idea of the big picture, you can work out the best way to put it into action. For example, you could use a lot of different, named bank accounts, jars on the kitchen bench (like they did in the old days) or envelopes. Sanity money could be in cash or in a separate bank account. Some people find it helpful to tally all their annual bills (rates, insurance, school fees, etc.), divide them by 12 and put that amount into a separate bills' account to keep on hand.

You do, of course, have to do a little work in the beginning to know how much each of those amounts is. However, once you set it up it should be reasonably simple to manage on a long-term basis. I find automatic payments work best, because when you manually make transfers, it is harder to stick to your system, and you can easily change your automatic payments if your system needs to be tweaked.

Without a doubt, setting up a new money system can be the least enjoyable part of managing your money. But it is by far the most important thing you will ever do if you want to feel in control of your money and improve your financial situation. Especially if you are on a low income, you will have to watch your spending very closely, and the benefit of creating a detailed, manageable and effective system will be well worth the effort. For the most part, financially successful people don't get there by accident. They are very aware of how they spend, save and invest their money, and it all starts with having an effective money system.

Surveys show that people spend about 20% less when they pay cash instead of using credit. This is because it is more 'painful' to part with cash than hand over a card. When you pay cash, you tend to think more about what you are spending.

YOUR BUSINESS MONEY SYSTEM

In New Zealand we have one of the highest numbers of small business owners per capita in the world. One of the biggest challenges businesses face, especially small businesses, is managing their cashflow. Once your business gets large enough you usually have staff who specialise in this area, but until you get to that point, as a business owner you need to keep a tight handle on it. Below is a money system that is effective for smaller businesses.

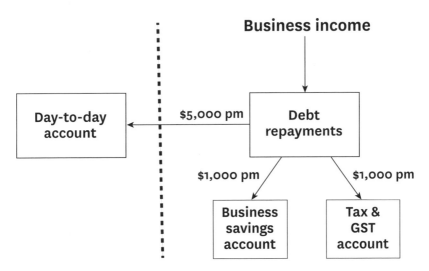

In this example $5,000 per month is paid into your personal account, which you would run in your personal money system along the lines of the three examples above.

Separating out your accounts

One of the most common issues I find with small businesses is that the owner treats their business income like their personal income. When you earn a dollar in your business you don't get to keep it all. Simple and obvious, I know — but time and time again I find that while business owners understand this, they don't put it into practice. A key reason is probably because they get used to spending as if they are earning all of the gross income and so they are constantly juggling money around to try to make it work.

I find the easiest way to manage this is to keep your personal and business finances completely separate. Imagine there is a brick wall between the two, and the only way that money goes between your business and personal accounts is via a planned and automatic process with notations, so you know what it was for. In the example above, $5,000 is paid from the business account to the personal account on a monthly basis.

Pay yourself an income

Essentially you and your business have an employer–employee relationship. This means that you pay yourself a regular income as if you were an employee. It doesn't matter if this is weekly, fortnightly or monthly. Whichever works for you is fine. Of course, you need to do a budget for your business and see what amount is appropriate to pay yourself as a salary. It's often best to start at a lower amount and then increase it as the business can comfortably afford it. Once you receive the income personally you need to go back to your personal spending plan (budget) and make that amount work.

Tax and GST

You can either pay tax on your personal income (salary/wages) as you go, which is called PAYE (pay as you earn), or put the equivalent amount into your tax and GST account and pay your provisional and terminal tax when they're due. These taxes can be defined as follows:

- **Provisional tax** is not a separate tax but a way of paying your income tax as the income is received through the year. You pay instalments at intervals, based on what you expect your tax bill to be. The amount of provisional tax you have paid is then deducted from your tax bill at the end of the year. There are currently three instalment (payment) dates. You can now pay your provisional tax payments on a regular basis. It's best to talk to your accountant about this so it is set up correctly.
- **Terminal tax** is the difference between what you have paid in provisional tax (if any) over the previous year and what it turns out you actually owe. If you have paid too little provisional tax, you must pay terminal tax, and if you have paid too much you get a refund.
- **GST (Goods and Services Tax)** is a tax added to most goods and services sold for consumption in New Zealand. It is paid by customers. If you have customers, you will charge 15% GST on the products or services you sell (GST collected) and be able to claim for the GST that you have paid on what you have purchased (GST credit). The difference between GST collected minus your GST credit is the amount you pay to the government, or (if the credit is greater), they may pay you. You don't have to register for GST unless you expect to have revenue over $60,000 per year.

If you are putting money aside for tax, just remember not to use the money in that account unless it's essential and if you have a well-thought-through plan to replace it. It is best to pretend it's not there. This is an area where many small businesses get into trouble as they often don't have enough money put aside to pay their tax bills. There is a lot of information and help on www.ird. govt.nz, and you can also ask your accountant to help you put the best system in place for your situation. If you mess around and fail to pay your tax, it will be the ruin of your business, so please be very proactive in this area. Revenue is important in a business but equally important is the actual after-expenses cashflow and the tax you pay on it. This effectively is the money you get to keep.

Savings

If you have a lot of money in your trading account, put it into your savings account, either in a lump sum or on a regular basis. It's also good to have some money set aside in case you need it for a quiet period in your business or if there are projects you want to take on. If you start to accumulate a lot of money in this account, you could transfer more over to your personal account or into investments. You could do this as drawings or a dividend but it's best to get advice from your accountant.

YOUR TOTAL MONEY SYSTEM

Below is what your entire money system would look like. Essentially, it's about separating the different parts of your financial life so you have a simple system that is easy to manage. You can modify it to find something that suits you best. For instance, if you don't have a business, any spare money in your personal savings account could go to extra mortgage or debt repayments or directly across to your long-term investment account.

You can manage your money system any way you want: on paper, spreadsheets, specialised software, or a combination of all of these. There is no right or wrong way — just find a solution that works best for you. When you begin, though, I recommend you draw a diagram of your system and money flow, as it's often easier to understand something that is visual. This is what I

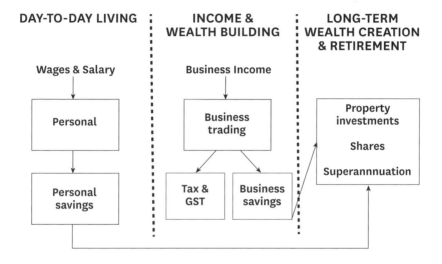

do with my clients. We create a draft in my office and then I encourage them to go home and think about what makes sense for their individual situation.

The short-term objective in creating your money system is to have more awareness and control around your money. Your long-term objective is to get funds across to the long-term wealth creation and retirement part of your financial life, and to build up assets. This helps you create more freedom and choice in your life — which is what this book is all about. The more assets you build up, the less you need to rely on earning a regular income.

Some helpful reminders

Helpful reminders to ensure your money system is effective:

- Match the frequency of your system to when you are paid: weekly, fortnightly or monthly.

- No bank is necessarily better than another. You may get discounted bank fees if you have a mortgage with a bank so just check out what is on offer.
- Sometimes people ask why you would have the extra bank accounts when you often have to pay fees. It is a good point. If having the additional accounts makes it much easier and more effective for you to manage your money, the additional fees is money well spent.
- Software systems can be helpful. PocketSmith is one of the popular ones and has been around for many years. If it helps you to use a specially designed system, use one. However, they are not necessary and many of my clients use a simple spreadsheet or keep track of things by hand. Whatever works for you is what is best.

'We are what we repeatedly do. Excellence then is not an act, but a habit.'

– ARISTOTLE

Case Study: Tips for saving money (Gillian — Hamilton)

Budgeting

When I was a stay-at-home mum, I decided that my job (besides raising kids!) was to be in charge of saving our family money while my husband focused on earning. I started by setting up a basic savings account and typed up a list of our regular payments: things like power, insurance and broadband, and reviewed our grocery spending. I sent each supplier an email explaining that we were happy customers but were down to one income to see if there was a better deal to be had. All of them (bar one) came back with suggestions for a different plan, package, or some form of discount. I ended up with over $4,000 in the savings account in the first year :-)

Every May, after the busyness of summer is over, I review our outgoings to see where we can trim costs. This year we cancelled our Sky subscription as we now watch less TV, which will save $1,200 a year. We've been with Sky for over 20 years and conservatively estimate it has cost us a staggering $18,000 over that time, which I shudder to think about.

I try to have a 'no-spend day' once a week, usually two days after payday — when my car's gas tank is full and I've done the weekly food shop, so I don't actually need to buy anything. I find lots of frittering-type purchases are done without thinking (takeaway coffee, magazines, vending machines) so by actively avoiding random spending one day a week you can save $50 to $60 a month.

Incremental investing

We have a very simple (but boring) investment strategy and that's to invest part of every pay cheque — even if it's a small amount. We have an automatic payment that deposits a set amount every Thursday into a low-fee, non-KiwiSaver investment fund. The amount we invest fluctuates from time to time and has been as low as $20 a week and as high as $200, but week by week it certainly adds up, and it's safely tucked away.

Reducing the mortgage

Without fail every time we refix our mortgage we increase our repayments, even if it's by just a few dollars. It's not a sophisticated strategy, but we're now hundreds of dollars ahead on our fortnightly repayments. When I returned to work, we were able to make a big increase, while other years it has just been an extra $10 or $20 a fortnight. It's a good way to quietly get ahead on your mortgage without missing the money. Times are tougher at the moment, so next year it may only be an extra $5 or so but it's still worth doing.

Decluttering

My best tip would be to do a massive house declutter and then set limits on the amount you own. Marie Kondo's book was life changing for me. I took her advice, which is to declutter by category, not room by room. We laid things out in groups, and were horrified to find how much excess stuff we owned, which we hadn't noticed because it was tidied away around the house. Random stuff, like over 40 baseball caps, hundreds of novels, 15 winter coats for just four of us and untold lunchboxes. Things that I've spent thousands of dollars on over the years. I have now set rough limits on the amount we own at any one time; for example, my kids have around 10 T-shirts each and five pairs of shorts, and one good-quality lunchbox each, with a spare one in the cupboard. I've noticed I shop (and therefore spend) a lot less and the house is infinitely easier to keep tidy.

Spending

Whenever I buy clothes, I use the '$1 per wear' rule of thumb to determine if it's good value or not. A $300 dress I'll wear to one or two weddings over summer works out to $150 per wear — not good value, whereas a $45 bra I'll wear 150 times over its lifespan or $100 jeans that I'll wear 200 times are good value. Even pricier items, like a $600 handbag, that I know I'll use 600 times (every day for two or three years) work out to be good value.

In a Nutshell

- Align your spending with your goals.
- When spending ask yourself if you really need it or do you simply want it?
- Develop a workable money system that is tailored to your needs.
- Make sure your money system is written down and not just in your head.
- Review it regularly.

STEP 3
Increase your income

THIS CHAPTER IS ALL ABOUT increasing your income — which of course we would all like to do, right? People rarely think they earn enough and always want more. Often, though, the more you earn, the more you spend. The bottles of wine, holidays, cars, clothes, eating out get more frequent and expensive so you do not end up better off.

You want to aim to get a bigger gap between what you earn and what you spend, as that is what gets you ahead. I always get my clients to complete a financial questionnaire before they come to see me and there is an income and expenditure form on it. Some complete it in detail and others think it's painful so just throw in some random numbers, often because they only want to talk to me about investing so don't perceive that information as useful. The reality is that for me to help them put a savings or investment plan in place we need to know what surplus funds they have to grow their wealth.

So, in short, the gap between what you earn and what you spend is really important. You can increase this gap by spending less and by increasing your income. My preferred strategy is to do both.

Money-saving tips

Let's start with the money-saving tips. Put your creative hat on and think about smart ways you can save money. If you are motivated, you will be amazed at how resourceful you can be.

CREATIVE SOLUTIONS

Here are some ideas.

Never pay retail

You will be surprised at what discounts you can get by just asking. Seek discounts and look for special offers, bulk deals and coupons. Look for items with damaged packaging, clearance items or bargain bins. Wait for the sales. For example, if you are going to be close to shops on Boxing Day, write a list of things you need in the months before and then brave the queues. It might be a bit of a scrum, but you can save a lot of money.

Become food smart

This is an area where you can make big savings and there are lots of ideas:

- Become a culinary genius — think outside the box with your cooking. It's amazing what delicious family meals can be made out of a stray tin of tuna, half a can of baked beans or the peanut butter at the bottom of the jar.
- Before shopping, build your menu for the week ahead, so you get the maximum use out of what you buy. Shop only once a week. Usually, the more we shop, the more we spend.
- Try walking around the edges of the supermarket when you shop and avoid the middle. This is because all the fresh food is usually on the outer aisles, and the items that you are tempted by and don't necessarily need are on the inner

aisles. This strategy can also be great for your health.

- What do you have stored in your cupboard or freezer that you didn't know you had?
- Give yourself a set amount each week to use for the groceries so you don't overspend. Alternatively, take cash. You might have to take a calculator with you so you know how much you are spending.
- Buy in-house brands or plain packs — they almost always cost less than the other brands and are usually of similar quality.
- Double up when cooking some of your meals so you can freeze them for when you don't feel like cooking or take it for lunches the next day.
- Try companies like My Food Bag. They may seem expensive but if it reduces waste and the number of takeaways you buy, you will save money. They can also reduce the stress of worrying about what to cook for dinner and give you great ideas for other meals.
- Make and take your lunch to work rather than buying it at the local cafés.
- Limit yourself on bought coffees — say, one a day or a week. For the price of four of them, you could buy a whole kilo of fresh grounds.
- Reduce or cut out takeaways. Cooking at home is not only cheaper but also healthier.
- If you are going to be out for a while, pack snacks and drinks so you don't have to buy them at the shops. Think also of how many plastic bottles you won't consume.
- Watch TV shows like *Eat Well for Less* for ideas.

Eat out well for less

- Buy vouchers from discount sites like First Table or GrabOne. You can get some amazing deals and you have the chance to eat out in places where you may not normally go. Be mindful, though, not to get hooked on discount fever and end up buying more than you wanted to.
- Have fewer drinks when you eat out as they add a lot to your bill.
- Take turns having dinner at friends' places or have potluck-style dinners.

Shop well

- Shopping at a supermarket when you are hungry often leads to excessive spending.
- Don't go to the mall or the shops when you feel bored or need a pick-me-up. Your purchases may make you feel great at the time, but the feeling rarely lasts. Buy used. New is nice, but for the best buys think pre-owned or pre-loved, whether it's from Trade Me or your local op shop.
- When choosing gifts for people, buy on sale or consider making them, such as baking or homemade cards.
- When buying bigger-ticket items, shop around: the saving margins can be significant. Sales like Black Friday and Boxing Day can offer some great deals.
- Borrow, trade or swap with people for things you need, such as clothing and toys for kids.
- Save electricity by turning off any unused appliances. See www.powerswitch.org.nz for tips on cutting power bills and switching to a cheaper provider.
- If you like going to the movies, most cinemas have a night when the tickets are cheaper.

- For a lower-cost holiday, consider swapping your house with someone for a couple of weeks.

Plan ahead

Planning ahead almost always will save you money. Use a shopping list so you don't buy things you don't really need. I have friends who do most of their shopping online as not only is it convenient but they think it saves them money as they are not as tempted to buy excess things.

Be less wasteful

The wastage we create is huge and it is a real issue for our planet. Many of us throw away an enormous amount of food and other general stuff each week that just goes into landfill.

Bulk deals

If you have a large freezer, buy vegetables when they are in season as you can buy them cheaper, and freeze them. Be careful not to buy more than you need though. While buying three heads of broccoli may seem tempting, if you can't use them before they go bad you are wasting rather than saving money.

Grow

Become a gardener — this is more long term, but increasing numbers of people are going back to some of the basics. Even if you grow your greens and herbs, you can save a lot of money and eat more healthily in the process. Trade any extra produce you have with someone else.

Learn

Google 'money-saving tips'. There are literally thousands of ideas online. Chat with your friends and family. I think this is an especially good idea and doing it regularly brings attention to ways to save money.

THE $10 PER WEEK GROCERY CHALLENGE

This is an interesting exercise. The original concept was a $21 per week challenge ($5.25 per person), created by Australian Fiona Lippey, the founder of Simple Savings (www. simplesavings.co.nz), a very successful money-saving website.

Given she came out with the idea many years ago and inflation has had an impact, I've used $10 per week per person. Assume you have no income for the week. Now imagine you have $40 (assuming a family of four) in the bank left for groceries. How are you going to survive? Give the Grocery Challenge a go! Pretend it's like the reality show *Survivor*, but instead of going away to some remote location you are stuck in your kitchen with only your pantry, fridge and freezer to help you. Most people think I've gone completely mad when I suggest this concept and are adamant that it can't be done. Yet, many thousands of people have successfully completed the challenge, with incredibly rewarding results.

The challenge is not intended for every week but for one week only, although you can repeat it as often as you like. Ideally you spend the money on perishable items like bread, milk, fruit and vegetables and then get resourceful and creative using what is in your cupboards.

Based on the average weekly spend of $300 for a family of four, doing this challenge say four times per year can save you $1,040 on the annual food bill. This extra money could help with unexpected bills or just help you save some money. It's great to do it closer to Christmas and be able to put some extra money away for the holidays.

There are literally endless opportunities to save money.

Put your thinking cap on and go for gold! It's sometimes just a matter of stopping and thinking before you spend. While you might save only a few dollars here and there, you will be amazed at how much it adds up to over time.

For instance, if you cut back on buying an average of one coffee a day:

$5 x 7 days = $35 per week

$35 x 52 weeks = $1,820 per year

If you keep that up for 10 years, it will save a staggering $18,200. If you invest that money instead at, say, 5% per annum you will have approximately $28,679 in savings. And are you sitting down? If you invested that for 20 years, it's a whopping $75,614. Welcome to the world of compounding interest, which we will explore in Chapter 5.

Remember you only get to spend your hard-earned dollars once, so you want to get the most benefit possible from them. Go forth and get resourceful and creative in your ways to save money!

Ways to increase your income

Now that we have looked at ways to increase the gap between what you earn and what you spend by being smarter spending your income, let's look at some different ways to increase your income. Bear in mind, though, not to increase your spending to match your new income, otherwise you are right back where you started. Remember your aim is to improve your financial position.

CREATIVE SOLUTIONS

Upskilling

Continuing to improve your skills can lead to your income increasing over time. Investigate things you can do to make yourself more employable. Look at courses, talk to your manager about how you can add more value in your job, and ask if there is any training they will support you doing.

Ask for a pay rise

Are you getting paid market rates for what you do? If you are doing a good job, maybe you could ask for a salary review. First, do some research so you are well aware of market rates. Also give some thought to how you plan to approach your employer and show them that you really do deserve the increase in your pay and the value that you create in the business. Don't just assume that because you ask, you will get one. Of course, if you don't ask, you will never know . . .

Overtime

Will your company allow you to do some overtime? Even if it is only occasional, it all adds up. Or there might be an extra job you can take on with your current employer. For instance, they might need an extra resource for a few hours a week or on the odd occasion to pick up a specific task.

Side hustles

Turn your skills into cash. What about getting an extra job working at night or in the weekends — for instance, in a bar or restaurant, or in retail. This was one of the ways I personally got ahead financially in my early days. What skills do you have that could bring in extra income? Ask around and tell people you are available. The list is endless:

- If you can cook well, can you sell home baking (cakes, preserves, pies) to your friends and family or at local fairs or markets?
- If you are a handyman, can you do some odd jobs for your neighbourhood?

- Babysit. Most of the people I know with young children find it hard to get a good babysitter.
- Think local — do your neighbours need someone to wash windows, clean, dog walk, tutor, babysit . . . ?
- Become an extra on a film set or a mystery shopper.
- Did you know you can get paid for doing online surveys?
- Local companies like www.sidekicker.com/nz/ specialise in hiring temporary and casual staff.
- For an international focus see companies like www.upwork.com, www.fiverr.com and www.freelancer.com
- Use your car for cash and drive part time with Uber or Zoomy or Ola.

Sometimes your side hustle can turn into very successful businesses. Pure Delish started life as a seasonal festive cake company in 1997. The business was founded by Kaz Staples, a young mum who decided she needed to make some extra cash for her family at Christmas. Being a keen baker, for Kaz this seemed like a logical way to generate income. She saw a gap in the market for high-end Christmas cakes and decided to fill it. With some 40 products, 30 staff and a thriving business later, Pure Delish is a real Kiwi success story.

Rent your space

Do you have an extra room or two to take in a boarder or student? The overseas students (particularly in the main centres) pay $300 to $350 per week for full board. If you are okay with having people around, this can be a good way to create extra income. Airbnb could be another good option. Some of my clients have really found this extra income helpful and often use the money for a special purpose like extra mortgage payments, a family holiday, renovations or investing. Although many wouldn't necessarily choose to rent out their spare space, they reconcile it with benefits they are getting.

Trading tasks

Are there things that you can trade with someone else? While it won't pay you, it could save you spending money, which amounts to more or less the same thing. A recent example I came across was a grandmother who was struggling with money. Her children were doing okay financially, so they cut a deal whereby they mowed her lawns on a regular basis in return for her babysitting her grandchildren for no compensation.

House sitting

I've had clients over the years who have been full-time house sitters. This has enabled them to save a lot of money. Some do it for a few years to save for a specific thing like a house deposit, while others enjoy the variety and do it long term. You may need to have friends or family to stay with for the odd week here and there when you don't have a house to sit, but in my experience it's rarely needed.

Sell stuff

Most of us have stuff around the house that we never use. Have you looked at having a garage sale? Maybe you can organise one for your neighbourhood and take a percentage of the profits. What about selling things on websites like Trade Me or eBay? We renovated recently and I sold heaps of things on Trade Me. I also gave away a lot of stuff free, which made me feel better about limiting the amount going into landfill. I laughed at my partner selling a very old tool box that I said he was dreaming if he thought anyone was going to pay money for. Well, he had the last laugh as he got $340 for it. Apparently, it was a rare local brand.

Check the detail

Read every statement and bill. Question every discrepancy and make sure you are not paying for someone else's mistakes. I personally have picked up incorrect charges on my phone bill, credit card and bank statements. Twice I've had large amounts occur on my credit card that were not my purchases. Often, it's only small amounts, but it all adds up.

Pay your bills on time

A number of organisations — for example, power and phone companies — will give you discounts if you pay on time. Others will charge you extra if you *don't* pay on time. Keep an eye on bill deadlines so you pay the minimum. I set up all my payments on direct debit. It saves me time and I don't need to worry about remembering to pay on time.

HELP FROM THE GOVERNMENT

Have you contacted the relevant government organisations to see what financial assistance you are entitled to? There are a number of payments that are available. Here are some of the main ones:

Family assistance

Working for Families tax credits are payments for families with dependent children aged 18 and under. The payments are to help you raise your family. Entitlements are based on your yearly family income and family circumstances.

Best Start payment

This is a weekly payment for a child's first year. It is not income tested and is eligible for all children. If the family income meets the criteria, it may be extended until the child is three.

Accommodation supplement

The accommodation supplement is delivered by Work and Income and you may be eligible, depending on where you live, your income, assets and housing costs. You may qualify for assistance with your rent, board, mortgage and essential housing costs.

Childcare subsidy & OSCAR (Out of School Care and Recreation) subsidy

Work and Income provide financial support to help families with the costs of before- and after-school care for up to 20 hours a week, and school holiday programmes for up to 50 hours a week. The amount you receive depends on the size of your family, your income, and how many hours a week your child goes to the childcare provider. All subsidies are paid directly to the childcare provider.

> **Did you know?** There are approximately 560,000 businesses operating in New Zealand. Nearly 75% of them have no employees and nearly 20% have one to five employees. We are an entrepreneurial nation and have one of the highest rates of business ownership per capita in the world.

START YOUR OWN BUSINESS

Many people dream of having their own business and becoming their own boss. It can be a great way to get ahead financially. It may be that your side hustle takes off and you want to put more focus into growing it. Or you may decide to purchase an existing business. The decision to have your own business should not be made lightly, though, as 75% of businesses fail in the first four years. So, what are the pros and cons of running your own company, and what do you need to know?

Advantages
- You are your own boss — so you can work whatever hours you like and leverage your time.
- You can work from home.
- You could make big profits.
- You control your own income.
- There are tax advantages in working for yourself.

Disadvantages
- Clients will dictate how you operate.
- You'll probably need to work 60–80 hours per week for the first few years.
- In the beginning you may make very little money or even make a loss.
- You could get ripped off.
- You carry all the responsibility, and the process can be lonely and worrying.
- Until you can afford help, you'll be doing everything.
- There can be risk and legal liability issues to consider.

There are lots of different ways of getting into business, but ultimately you need to either come up with an idea yourself or buy into an existing business. Buying into an existing business may have less risk, but it will most likely require more funding. If you're beginning from scratch, you will need to do some market research and due diligence to make sure there is a market for your business and, most importantly, whether you can make money from it. I have seen lots of great business ideas, but many don't do that well financially. It is also important to find a business that utilises your skills and experience and which you will enjoy, because the first few years could be pretty tough.

Write a business plan

Far too few people write a business and marketing plan before they launch into business. The old saying that 'If you don't know where you are going any path will get you there' is very true. You don't need to write a novel, but you do need to cover the key areas of your business. Your plan should include things like:

- Your concept or idea
- Your vision and objectives
- Branding and marketing
- Strengths and weaknesses of your business
- Opportunities or threats in the market
- Key relationships, customers, strategic alliances
- Costs, cashflow and funding
- Resources (staff, technology, stock)
- Your team (lawyer, accountant, financial advisor, business mentor, banker/funder)

Having your own business requires a lot of self-motivation and discipline. Some things are going to work and some are not. Think about how you will support yourself financially while the business is getting established. Have a financial safety net, which may look like having a chunk of cash set aside to cover your personal expenses until the business can pay you. There will undoubtedly be tough times, and if you're to ride through them you will need to be passionate about what you are doing and totally focused on your objectives.

In my experience many business owners in the short term can work twice as hard, earn half the amount and have three times the stress they did when they worked for someone else. It can be a lot of hard work and the buck stops with you! But if you love what you do, and if you stick with it and get it right, it can be incredibly rewarding and offer great financial benefits.

Case Study: Side gigs and lessons learned (Paul — Tauranga)

I came out of the military after many years. While I liked the people I worked with, I got rather sick of being told what to do and I was determined to forge my own path.

I was interested in learning how to make money online, but I had few or no skills except for an interest and an action mindset. I invested in courses and products that I thought could help me, most from the USA. Many were very good, but I didn't have the business skills and soon found myself with $10,000 in credit card debt. I also realised that I don't make very good decisions when under financial pressure.

I had a job, but I needed to find a side gig that would help me get rid of the debt. The job allowed me to live day to day, but I just needed some extra income. I then began my side gig journey:

Job One — washing rental cars. I could get through three cars in an hour (inside and out). While it was great as I got to work on my own, and could come and go as I wanted, keeping up momentum was difficult as I would get up to 12 cars a night.

Job 2 — pizza delivery. While this job did help me clear my debt it was very stressful. One day I arrived early and was working with the owner. I was the only other person in the shop as it was before the shift started.

The phone started to ring flat out, and after that it was call after call after call. My boss became more and more stressed as the workload increased and started yelling and swearing at me. I tried my best and was working as fast as I could, but I was clearly not meeting the grade.

Let's say, in the end I took off my apron and never went back.

Job 3 involved setting up and selling dog clothes online. I

was doing this in between working as a breakfast chef (from 3.55 am until 1.30 pm), training in martial arts for a black belt and educating myself in between times about Google advertising and rankings, website conversions and analytics.

Despite the crazy schedule, it was something I was passionate about and it led to being paid to speak at events to help others undertaking the same journey.

So, what did I learn from my side gigs?

- Clear your debts and never go back.
- Work your way into something you are interested in — you will be spending a lot of time doing it, so you need to enjoy it.
- You will make mistakes but ask yourself what you can do better next time.
- Take responsibility for the position you are in. I had got myself into debt and I needed to find a way out, so blaming others wouldn't help.
- Understanding and taking control of your financial situation is really empowering.

In a Nutshell
- Increase the gap between what you earn and spend.
- Make a list of areas where it is easiest for you to save money.
- Brainstorm ways to increase your income.
- Imagine yourself as a saver rather than a spender.

STEP 4
Decimate your debt

YOUR VIEW OF DEBT will have a major influence on how you take control of your finances. Debt is becoming increasingly ingrained into our culture. We now live in a cashless society where it is so easy to put everything on credit. Many people get to the end of the month and don't realise what they have put on credit through the month.

I have a very strong view on consumer debt, which is that you should avoid it like the plague or in these times maybe I should say Covid! It may sound like a harsh viewpoint but show me a financially successful person who has this debt. Besides making you feel awful, debt is your main barrier to building a financially secure future. Those who are comfortable with consumer debt will always struggle to get their personal finances under control. Debt should be a helpful tool to assist you to leverage yourself ahead financially, like to buy a home, help you study and get a qualification, start a business or purchase an investment property. Unfortunately, many people use it to buy consumables or to help with regular expenses. It has the effect of spending future money now and can significantly hold you back. It's also a method to make banks and finance companies wealthy, but not you.

The problem is that many people don't have the discipline to manage their credit effectively. For example, surveys suggest that there are more credit card holders that *don't* pay off their balance in full each month than there are those that do. Debt has a very nasty sting in its tail. You may feel great short term; however, those feelings may turn stressful quickly once you have to deal with paying the borrowing back. Savers will always be wealthier than spenders.

A great philosophy to live by is: If you can't pay cash for it, you can't afford to buy it.

Debt has many faces

The type of debt that I am concerned about is consumer debt. This is all debt you incur except for your mortgage on your own home or investment debt (i.e. debt on an asset that makes you money). Just to clarify, cars are not an investment. I have had a few clients over the years try to justify their car purchase as an investment, but unless you are in the business of buying and selling cars, you are out of luck — it's not an investment.

TYPES OF DEBT

Let's look at the various types of debt:

Overdraft

An overdraft is a loan provided by a bank that allows you to pay for bills and other expenses when your account reaches zero. It's a flexible facility as you only pay what you owe. Most banks will have a monthly account fee, plus a base rate fee of approximately 13% for anything owed, and if you go over your overdraft limit, an additional fee of around 5–6%.

Personal loans

These are provided by banks and finance companies. There is a plethora of options, and you can pay anything from 7% to 30% in interest depending on the level of security you have. The riskier the lender thinks you are, the higher the interest rate you pay. There may be additional fees like application fees or early repayment fees.

Credit cards

Credit cards are probably the most common type of consumer debt. They generally have an interest rate of around 20%, while some charge as much as 25%. You can get low-interest cards around 13%, but they come with no perks like airport lounge vouchers and travel insurance. These can be a better option if you really have to use credit and cannot pay off your balance each month. Many lenders will offer an interest-free period as enticement to get you to move your credit card to them. These are a great option to help you pay off your debt faster, but they only work as a temporary solution.

Store cards

A store card is a credit card that you can only use in one store or group. The Farmers Card is a good example. Like a credit card, you can use a store card to buy things on credit and pay them off at the end of the month or in stages to spread the cost. And just as with a credit card, you'll be charged interest if you don't repay in full each month.

Hire purchase

A hire purchase is when you buy something and pay for it later. You can take the item home right away and pay for it in instalments over a period. There is normally an interest-free period, such as 12 months, and then interest is charged after that.

Buy now pay later

Buy now pay later schemes like Afterpay, Zip, Laybuy or Genoapay are offered by many stores and allow you to pay off an item over several weeks interest free, on the basis that the scheduled payments are made on time. If they are not, fees are charged which can be quite significant. These schemes have become very popular in recent years and are becoming a real problem for many people so exercise caution.

Student loans

If you are studying (following high school), you can apply for a student loan. When you start working and earning over a certain threshold, repayments will be deducted from your income. While you are in New Zealand student loans are interest free. Try to make sure your loan is being used for course costs and living costs, not discretionary spending, otherwise it can start mounting up. Investing in your education can be very worthwhile; however, take care and minimise how much you borrow as you still need to pay it back.

Car loans

Car debt is one of the most common forms of personal debt. Often having an expensive car with a large loan is luxury and is more about image than it is about getting you around. Ask yourself — is the value of having an expensive car worth the stress of taking on such a big financial commitment? Interest rates vary between 5% and 25% depending on how secure you are perceived by the lender, similar to a personal loan. You can often get quite cheap interest when you buy a new car from a car dealer, but the trade-off is how much the car depreciates in value in the first few years.

> **Did you know?** If you buy a car worth $40,000 and pay, say, 10% interest on the loan over a four-year term, you will pay back a total of $48,690 for the car including interest. New cars depreciate about 40% in the first few years so at the end of four years you will have an asset worth half of what you paid for it. You have to want a new car pretty badly to want to lose that much money in such a short amount of time.

I am not outlining the various options to encourage you to take on debt, rather so you are aware that there are so many options available to entice you to borrow. These organisations make an enormous amount of money. Credit is incredibly convenient. If you are smart and plan what you buy, some of these credit options can be really useful. For instance, using a credit card and paying off the balance each month or taking out a hire purchase and paying it off during the interest-free period. The challenge is you are often tempted to buy things that you don't need or spend more than you have. And, of course, you still have to pay the money back.

Make a plan to blast your debt

If you haven't managed to escape the credit culture and have become a slave to your credit card and other debts, you now need to make a plan to pay it all off.

1. AVOID FUTURE DEBT

The first step in getting on top of your debts is to stop spending on credit. You are not going to make much headway decreasing your debts if you get more of them as fast as you pay off what you already have. If possible, if you can't afford to buy something without using credit, don't buy it. While this may feel a bit painful at first, many people find that the items they've been buying on credit are wants, rather than needs, and might not be as important or useful as they first thought. Save and pay cash for the things you want.

> **Did you know?** If you borrowed $10,000 on an average interest rate of 20%, you would pay $2,000 in interest each year if you didn't pay off your debt. So, in effect, not paying off your debt means the price you are paying is 20% more than the ticket price. That amount will increase each year that you don't pay off your debt.

Can you do without a credit card?

Credit cards can be incredibly convenient. They can also be one of your biggest problems when it comes to gaining control of your spending. It's just too darn easy to use them. Be honest with yourself: do you really need credit cards? Are they way too dangerous in your hands?

Many people have a number of credit cards. If you have one for business and one for personal use, that's a little different; but there are few reasons you should need more than one. Pick up a card and ask yourself whether you really need it. If the answer's *no*, take the scissors to it. If you decide *yes*, and find it a little difficult managing your spending, here are some tips on finding the right card for you.

- Read the terms and conditions carefully to check whether the card is the right type for your needs.
- Set a spending limit that suits your budget.
- Know what the interest rate is.
- Always pay off the balance every month to avoid paying interest.
- Only put on your card what is in your budget.
- Consider using a debit card instead. With a credit card, you're borrowing money to be repaid later. When you use a debit card, the money is deducted from your day-to-day account, so it allows you to spend only what you have.
- Don't take your card shopping with you (you can always go back if it's important), or lock it away and use it only for emergencies.

If your credit card is really letting you down, you may need to consider chopping it up. A less drastic option may be to give your card to a close friend or family member for safe keeping, on the instruction that they give it back to you only when you have paid off your debts or in the case of an emergency. You can put it in a container of water and leave it in the freezer, so you have to defrost it before you need it. Seriously! This has worked well for people. Ultimately, there is no right or wrong way; eventually you'll find a solution that works for you.

Note: *Credit cards are okay if you pay them off in full every month. Just avoid getting into bad habits and stay aware of exactly what you are spending.*

What about reward points?
Reward points are a great bonus, but that's all they are. Companies spend enormous amounts of money developing and

running various loyalty schemes whose sole focus is, obviously, to get you to spend more money. Purchasing something that you don't necessarily need just to get reward points is, when you think about it, a false economy. Why buy something to get a 1–2% discount towards a future purchase or gift? If you are already planning to buy an item and you have budgeted for it, and it so happens that you get reward points, that's a nice bonus. Every little bit adds up and these reward points can be a good way of saving you money — but only if you genuinely need the item and are not buying it just for the sake of a bit of retail therapy or accumulating points.

Don't worry about the Joneses

Curse those high-living, debt-ridden Joneses. If they get a new car, we have to get a new car. If they put a swimming pool in the backyard or get a new kitchen, so must we. If they go on an expensive European holiday, we must follow.

No doubt you have heard the saying 'keeping up with the Joneses'. It was originally the title of a comic strip by Arthur R. (Pop) Momand, which ran in many US newspapers from 1913 to 1938. Pop based the strip on his own experiences in suburbia, where the neighbours were in constant competition for the smartest house, garden and so on. So, the phrase has come to describe the practice of competing to maintain an appearance of affluence and wealth for the benefit of others. It's an easy trap to fall into, but it's also ruinous.

Don't be fooled by what you perceive other people have. I have seen many people over the years that have the big incomes, expensive cars, houses in the best suburbs and the latest designer clothes, but underneath it all they have very little net worth and are drowning in debt.

I think in today's world social media has made it even harder to keep a reality check on our spending. We are constantly bombarded with glossy images. If Kim Kardashian recommends something, you need to have it. It's very easy to get caught up in what you think others have.

Some of the temptations might be:

- Having a home in an expensive suburb that you can't really afford
- Upgrading your cars every few years
- Overseas or expensive holidays
- Private education for your children
- Being seen in the right places, such as fancy restaurants
- Being label-obsessed
- Having lots of stuff that you never use
- Always wanting to look like you can be on the cover of a magazine

The truth is that, unless you are one of only two people in the entire world, there will always be people who are better off than you and some who are worse off than you. Get used to it and don't worry about what everyone one else is doing. Rather than getting caught up in the perceived status of having things you can't really afford, think instead about the freedom you will have when you have paid off your mortgage and have a debt-free home, or can afford to work part time, do a job you love rather than one that is paid more, or can retire earlier.

2. MAKE A LIST

Before you work out a plan for getting rid of your debt, you need to establish your starting point by working out exactly what you owe. How wonderful it would be to hear the word *nothing*! Once you get to the end of this exercise you will be able to say that. Interestingly, not many people know how much they owe in total. I guess because it's pretty scary and you think you are better off not knowing! This can be a tough step as what you owe is now staring you in the face. Knowledge is empowering so get brave and complete the table below to work out what your starting point is. Remind yourself how amazing you will feel when you do this exercise in the future and you have nothing to put on your list.

Type of debt	Interest rate	Total owed	Monthly payment	Annual payment	Total interest cost
Credit cards					
Store cards (e.g. Farmers Card)					
Hire purchases					
Car loans					
Family loans					
Student loan					
Buy now pay later loans					
Other					
TOTAL		$	$	$	$

3. MAKE A PLAN

Now you have stopped charging and adding to your total debts and know how much you owe you need to put a workable plan in place to pay off all of your debts. There are two ways to do this:

Debt avalanche method

This method is based on putting all of your extra money into the debt with the highest interest rate and fees first. Once that is paid off then you tackle the one with the next highest interest rate. Then rinse and repeat until you've paid them off and they all come down in an avalanche.

Pros	Cons
· Minimises the amount of interest you pay · Decreases the amount of time it takes to get out of debt · Good for budget-oriented people	· Takes discipline and commitment to pull off · Requires consistent amount of discretionary income

Debt snowball method

This method focuses on paying off the smallest debt first. The theory is that you reduce the total amount of debts you have quicker. It may cost more in interest but it's more motivating. You gain momentum, pick up speed like a snowball, and get the motivation you need to keep going.

Pros	Cons
· Builds motivation by reducing the number of debts faster · Easy to implement	· More expensive overall as incurs more interest · Can take longer to become completely debt free

Both methods involve you continuing to pay the minimum payments on each debt first as you don't want to occur any additional fees.

Finding the funds

Whichever method you think will work best for you relies on you finding the extra money you need to pay more than the minimum payments. The options are:

- Go back to your money system in Chapter 2 and review the options in Chapter 3. Ideally you want to find an amount that you can regularly contribute to your debts.
- Whenever you receive additional income from a tax refund, gift, raise, or the like, commit it to debt repayment. Since you hadn't planned on this income, you won't miss it.
- Dig into savings. If you have some money stashed away in a low-interest account (such as a savings account), think about using it to pay down some debt. Your savings account is only paying you a very small interest rate, but you're paying much more than that on your debt. Make sure you still have money in your emergency account.

Consolidating your debts

When faced with mounting debts from several creditors, you might feel the easy solution is to lump them all into a single debt-consolidation loan at a lower all-round interest rate. But is this a good idea? The answer is that it depends, and I have mixed views on whether it works. It can save you money if you get the right mix of interest rate and time frame; however, people often fail to consider both factors together, and instead look at the interest rate only. The easiest way to explain this is to look at the example below:

Type of loan	Loan amount	Interest rate	Period of loan	Payment per month	Interest paid
Low-interest credit card	$10,000	5%	6 months	$1,691	$145
Mortgage	$10,000	7%	25 years	$71	$11,218
Secured personal loan	$10,000	15%	4 years	$278	$3,355
Credit card	$10,000	19.95%	4 years	$304	$4,589
Unsecured personal loan	$10,000	25%	4 years	$331	$5,907

Note: *I've made a number of assumptions in these examples. While current mortgage rates are lower than 7%, I have used that figure because it's closer to the longer-term average. It will be helpful for you to do your own table to compare the best option for your individual situation.*

Balance transfer credit card

These are usually offered as a marketing exercise to attract new customers so it's unlikely you will get this from your current lender. It's when you get a new credit card which takes the balance from an existing card. In the process, you owe the new credit card the money, and the existing card is repaid. The new credit card will have a low interest rate, often 0%. The catch is that you only get this interest rate for a set period, usually six to 12 months. You may be charged a one-off transfer fee of around 1–2% and an annual fee for the new card. Ideally, you want one with a small transfer fee and a long low-interest rate period so that you maximise the savings available.

Balance transfer credit cards are a fast way to clear debts as they enable you to pay the debt off faster because you're not paying interest on top. Ideally, get rid of your old credit card or lower the credit limit so you can still use it for emergencies. You don't want to be tempted to use it and get more debt.

Low-interest credit cards

Many banks offer low-interest credit cards. It may not make sense to change banks and transfer your balance, but you could look at what lower-interest rate cards are available. Low-interest credit cards are around 13% instead of 20% interest. They don't offer any frills, but they can save you money while you are paying them off.

Using your mortgage

Adding your consumer debt to your mortgage can also be a great option, but the caveat is the time frame. I've come across many people who have been really pleased with themselves for getting a lower interest rate than, say, their credit cards, but the debt is put into a revolving-credit type facility which they may or may not pay off, or onto their current mortgage, which often has a long time frame of maybe 25 years. As you can see from the table above, even though the interest rate is low, the total interest paid is almost double the next most expensive. Using your mortgage *can* save you a lot of interest if you get a separate mortgage for a specific time frame (a few years, say) that meets the payment plan you have worked out.

Personal loans

These often have some of the highest interest rates depending on how secure the lender perceives you to be. You usually have set payments over a set time frame and are forced to be disciplined in payments, which for many people is really important — so maybe it is worth paying the higher interest rates.

Credit cards

Apart from the low-interest cards, most have an interest rate of approximately 20%. They are probably too flexible to be useful for debt consolidation as you can easily take out more credit and only have to pay the minimum amount off each month. If you are disciplined and have a plan that consolidates your debts to save interest, it can be a very effective financial option for paying off your debts cheaper and quicker. The devil, of course, is always in the detail, and not many of us are very disciplined. (It would be fair to assume that if you have a lot of consumer debt, discipline may not be your strong point.)

Finding a debt consolidation option where you are locked into payments is probably the best way forward, so long as you remove access to your credit cards so you don't add more debt as fast as you pay it off. I've seen plenty of examples where people have consolidated their debts into a personal loan or their mortgage and then maxed out their credit cards again, consolidated again, and then repeated the process a few more times, only to end up drowning in oceans of debt.

4. TRACK YOUR PROGRESS

Tracking your progress is a really important part of your debt-repayment journey. Not only does it show how much headway you are making but it can be incredibly motivating to see those debts being blasted away. You could track your progress in a diary, in a spreadsheet, or some of my clients have created quite elaborate visual charts which could be done electronically or with some good old-fashioned paper and coloured pens. This is especially good if you are a visual person. It could be really fun using your creative skills to develop something that is meaningful for you. Some important things to note are:

- Be in a place mentally where you really, really want to get rid of your debts and are very committed to the process.
- Set goals around your plan so you know what your targets are.
- Make sure your plan is practical and makes sense to you. The best plan is the one you like and that you feel will work for you.
- Put some rewards into your plan at key points along the way. Or do something special at the end when all your debts are paid off.
- You want to be able to clearly see your balances going down. Keep it front and centre so you are regularly reminded of where you are at.
- Get a support partner to keep you on track, motivate you when it gets tough and celebrate your successes along the way.

One of the most awesome things about paying off your debts is the change of habits and new money management skills you will have developed along the way. Imagine putting all this money you have been saving to pay off debts towards something that improves your wealth like a home or some investments. How cool would that be? I have seen many situations where people have been completely overwhelmed with the amount of debt they have and then have gone on to pay it off with hard work and determination. The lessons they have learned have been very valuable. So I know you can do it!

Case Study: Hard lessons in money management (Mel — Nelson)

It was exhilarating to finish high school and move away from home to another city when I went to university in 2005. The banks at that time were giving out credit cards to students like candy, with automatic credit limit increases every year. My increasing student loan meant I became desensitised or numb to the credit card debt. I had various part-time jobs throughout my years of study, primarily babysitting, so I always felt that everything would be fine because I had some money coming in. The credit card was my main form of payment and it was increasingly nearing its limit every month, despite my part-time job.

I bought an expensive sports car during that time mainly from saving up my student cost-of-living payments. I also bought lots of new things like an upgraded TV and an expensive hair straightener. Our flat would have 'takeaway buffets', getting a few different takeaways to enjoy at one meal.

I didn't have a plan for when I finished study. When my student life ended, I didn't know what to do so I found a job to tide me over while I worked it out. It took me a while to realise that my consumer spending was not helpful, and I wish I'd understood earlier how money worked so I hadn't wasted all the money I did and saved it instead.

It took me many years of learning how to manage my finances to get out of the habit of consumer spending, relying on credit cards and instead making regular savings and setting financial goals to work towards.

My boyfriend and I managed to scrape just enough deposit together to buy a house with our KiwiSaver funds. We had to sell the sports car, which was just a few years after the purchase and meant a loss of $7k. If we didn't have KiwiSaver, which forced us to save, we wouldn't have been able to buy a house.

We decided that buying a house was our priority and we made sacrifices by living with family, not going on overseas holidays, cutting our spending and focusing on increasing our earnings, as well as delaying having children. Everyone has different priorities, and you need to decide what works for you. Ignore what others are doing and make sacrifices in other areas to work towards your goals.

Something that hasn't come naturally for me as a woman is backing myself. I have had to learn how to silence my self-doubts and to speak up for myself, to have the confidence to try something different and face new challenges. This has meant applying for new jobs and asking for that pay rise. This is what has helped me grow my personal income.

More education at high school on managing budgets, debt and setting financial goals would be invaluable to help more young people get on the right foot when they go out into the real world.

It is primarily women who sacrifice their careers to grow their families, and this comes at a financial cost, especially if there is a relationship breakdown. It would be great to see more education and support for women to give them the knowledge, tools and confidence to understand, manage and grow their finances. This will be important if we are to close the gender inequality gap.

I'm now in my mid-thirties, married with a young son. We live in a lovely home, and I am happy. We have worked hard on having multiple income streams. We both work full time, we have flatmates to help with our mortgage, and we own an investment property. We are making contributions to investment funds to grow them with a view to hopefully retire a bit earlier. We also have got into a position where we can make regular donations to charity in order to help others.

I am very grateful for what we have achieved and feel positive about the future. It has been a long road of financial learning and skill development to get to this point and there is always something to work on. I also want to acknowledge that I have been privileged to grow up in a white middle-class family where my parents made some small financial contributions in the early days, but they made it clear to my sister and I that we needed to work things out ourselves.

Postscript

I have just been advised that my work contract will not be renewed and will finish at the end of the year. However, I feel comfortable that we are in a good position so that we will be able to manage until we are able to replace that lost income and work hard on our future goals again.

In a Nutshell

- Remember that debt is a noose around your neck and will always hold you back financially.
- If you have consumer debt, put a practical and sustainable plan in place to pay it off so you can then focus on building your financial wealth.
- Buying things on credit may make you feel good at the time but how does it make you feel when you are paying it off?
- Only put on credit what you have budgeted for and have a plan to pay it off.
- Be aware of the cost of credit — is this cost worth it to you?

STEP 5
Grow your wealth

NOW WE CAN START LOOKING at how to really grow your wealth. This wouldn't be possible without getting clear about what you want to achieve and figuring out how much you can save by working through the exercises in the previous chapters.

Smart savings

The terms 'saving' and 'investing' are often used interchangeably. Essentially, they are the same thing; however, I tend to use savings more in the context of a short- to medium-term time frame and investing more in the context of long term or for retirement. A lot of my view comes from experience with clients when I ask what they are doing with their savings. The responses are often along the lines of saving for a holiday, a new car or a major purchase. A lot goes into consumption, which is quite different to long-term saving or investing. Investing is more for the purposes of retirement funding or replacing income from your job or business at some point in the future. It is about financially looking after your future self.

- *Short-term savings* — usually for a specific short-term goal like a car, holiday, new furniture, home renovations. Or it could be for your emergency fund. Generally, it is for things that are consumed short term.
- *Medium-term savings* — saving for a home deposit is a good example of medium-term savings as it may take you a few years to save what you need. It could also be for significant home renovations or saving funds to start a business.
- *Long-term savings* — I always think of this as saving or investing for your retirement. The time frame is more likely to be 10 years plus.

Why does this distinction matter? It's really just about making sure you know the purpose of your saving. Otherwise, you may have a tendency to always end up spending what you save on things that don't move you forward financially. The first part of this chapter is about short- to medium-term savings and the second part is more about long-term investing. So let's look at the various steps to becoming a great saver. We did go through a lot of it in the previous chapters, but it is worth revisiting.

STEPS TO SAVING

1. Make a commitment
The first step in a successful savings programme lies in making a commitment. I think we would all agree that the more you want to do something, or the more important it is to you, the more likely you will be successful. So step 1 is all about getting your head in the right place and deciding you want to save.

2. Set a goal
The best way to make something happen — such as putting a

deposit down on your first home — is to set yourself a specific savings goal.

3. Check that it's achievable

Your goal has to be sensible, take account of unexpected expenses and be achievable.

4. Separate your savings to a different account or even a different bank

Say you decide you want to save $30,000 over the next three years. By contributing your weekly savings to a high-interest savings account yielding an after-tax return of around 2.5%, you will need to find approximately $180 per week from your budget. Your savings' targets could include repayment of debt, saving for retirement, or even saving for your next holiday. Always use a separate savings and investment account so you won't be tempted to spend the money. Naming your account can also be helpful as you are reminded of its purpose when you look at it. Having your savings account with a different bank means that when you look at your day-to-day banking online you don't see the money. You won't be tempted to say to yourself, 'I'll just borrow it and pay it back later'. Yeah — right!

Several years ago, I had a client who earned very good money. After completing a budgeting exercise, we established that she could easily save $1,500 per month and she really wanted to save for a house deposit. Checking in with her a few months later, she was saving but not long after she was spending it. I suggested she set up an account with a different bank, which she did. It didn't help her save. The next suggestion was naming her account *house deposit savings* — and, bingo, she was away. When she looked at using her savings for something else, she felt she was robbing herself. A few years later she became a homeowner.

The key to saving is to be consistent and then time will reward you. No matter how small the amount you save, it will make a difference and the better your financial future will be. One of my favourite sayings is 'How do you eat an elephant? A bite at a time'. In other words, even if your goals seem overwhelming, just start, even if it's small. Over time you can always increase the amount you save and before you know it you will achieve your goals.

For instance, if you were able to put just $25 per week — that's just five lattes — into an appropriate savings vehicle (like a managed growth fund) for 30 years and earn 5% net per year, your total savings and interest would now be worth $90,645! This is an excellent example of how committing to a regular savings plan and taking advantage of compounding interest over time can produce amazing results. But don't delay — begin today.

Where can you save?

When you are saving for a shorter period, say less than five years, you don't want to take on much risk as you may not have time for markets to average out if they do dip for any reason. Similarly, if you are saving for, say, a house deposit and have worked out that you will want the money in a specific time frame, like three years, you want to choose a low-risk product. The last thing you want to do is invest in the sharemarket and find that when you want your money the market is in a down period and your funds have dropped in value. Let's look at some common low-risk options.

HIGH-INTEREST SAVINGS ACCOUNT

This offers great flexibility in that you can make deposits (and withdrawals) whenever you like. However, the trade-off for that flexibility is that the interest rates are low. Typically, you would need to maintain a minimum balance — say, $5,000 — to get the higher interest rates, and there may be a small fee if you drop below this amount or if you make more than one withdrawal per month. They are designed to help you save but discourage withdrawals. This shouldn't be an issue as, of course, you won't be taking money out until you reach your target, will you?

TERM DEPOSIT

Term deposits will pay a higher interest rate than a bank account, but you can't make withdrawals until the end of the term, which can range from 30 days to five years. If you do break a term deposit, you lose the interest. The thing you need to be mindful of with term deposits is that you can't save into them on a regular basis. So, if you use them you would save into your bank account first, and every so often transfer the money to a term deposit that offers a time frame to match your specific savings goal. It might be that you end up with several term deposits if, for instance, you are saving for a home deposit.

OFFSET MORTGAGE

This is a home loan that uses the combined balance of your bank accounts and subtracts this from the balance of your home loan, so you only pay interest on the difference. While your minimum repayments will remain the same, more of each repayment goes towards paying off the principal part of your loan. For example, if you have a home loan of $500,000 and you offset $20,000 of it using your day-to-day and savings balances, you'll only pay interest on $480,000 of your home loan. You don't earn any interest on your savings as such, but you save interest on your mortgage, which has the same effect.

CASH MANAGEMENT TRUSTS

Cash management trusts are provided by banks and fund

management companies and are where the funds of individual unit holders are pooled, and the primary investment is in cash securities. They are based on a unit price basis, are also flexible, usually pay more than a bank account or term deposits and are generally considered a low-risk investment.

P2P LENDERS

Peer-to-peer lending, also known as crowd-lending, are online-based financial platforms that match borrowers to investors. Borrowers apply for loans via a P2P platform's website, and if they are approved, investors fund the loans, charging them an agreed-upon interest rate. Investments are for a set period and have different interest rates depending on the security of the borrower.

· · · · · · · · · ·

Whatever you choose, the sole purpose of the account should be for your specific financial goals. It's best to put aside your savings and forget about them until you need the money, otherwise you may be tempted to use the money for other things. Before you make your decision, consider:

- the interest you will earn
- the risk of the investment
- how long you commit your money for
- how easily you can access your money or not
- what fees there are if any

Take time to do your homework and shop around, so that you find a savings option that best suits your needs. The one with the highest interest rate may not necessarily be the best option for you. As a general rule of thumb, the higher the interest rate the higher the risk.

Investing for the long term

Legal residents of New Zealand aged over 65 and who have lived here for 10 years since the age of 20 (five of those years must have been since you turned 50) are eligible for New Zealand Superannuation. Starting in July 2024, however, this residency requirement is gradually increasing to 20 years by July 2042. Superannuation should cover most of your basic living costs, but on its own it will not be enough to fund your retirement. The table below illustrates the gap between what New Zealand Superannuation will cover and what various lifestyles will cost.

The difference between total expenditure and current rates of New Zealand Superannuation

	Type of retirement	Total weekly expenditure	NZ Superannuation after tax at the M rate	Difference
1-person household	No frills — metro	$781.07	$462.94	-$318.13
	No frills — provincial	$650.34		-$187.40
	Choices — metro	$1,107.12		-$644.18
	Choice — provincial	$1,217.84		-$754.90
2-person household	No frills — metro	$931.17	$712.22	-$218.95
	No frills — provincial	$800.38		-$88.16
	Choices — metro	$1,578.15		-$865.93
	Choice — provincial	$1,263.03		-$550.81

Source: Massey's New Zealand Financial Education and Research Centre Annual Retirement Expenditure Guidelines 2022.

As you can see, there is a gap between what Superannuation will fund and what you are likely to spend. However, I think the lifestyles used in their research are pretty basic. If you like to dine out, have a lot of hobbies, want private health insurance or like to travel, you will need to fund a much bigger gap. Either way, you will need to fund some of your retirement and that's why it is essential to save for the long term yourself.

Before we look at the various investment options available to help you save for the long term, let's explore some key principles.

COMPOUNDING INTEREST

The power of compounding is possibly the most understated concept when investing. Compounding interest is simply earning interest on interest. Albert Einstein said that compounding interest is the 'greatest force in the universe' and the 'eighth wonder of the world'. Over time it is incredibly powerful so never underestimate its impact.

The best way to make the most of compounding interest is to start early. The earlier you begin investing, the more years you earn interest and, as a consequence, the larger the investment base and the interest on it becomes. The following table shows how growth tends to accelerate over time. Look, for instance, at how much interest you earn and how much you amass in total if you start saving at the age of 20 instead of, say, at 40.

Saving $100 per month at 5% p.a. compounded monthly (tax of 30%) by 65 years old

Starting age	Amount contributed	Interest earned	Total savings
20	$54,000	$76,960.46	$130,960.46
30	$42,000	$40,220.64	$82,220.64
40	$30,000	$17,856.76	$47,856.76
50	$18,000	$5,628.60	$23,628.60
60	$6,000	$546.61	$6,546.61

Time and savings are the friends of compounding
The benefits of compounding aren't realised overnight. Patience is required. The key is to hang on in there. Often when you are starting it doesn't seem like you are making a lot of progress, but, as can be seen above, the returns really start accelerating the longer you keep investing. You *must* reinvest the interest and add it to your capital base if you want to reap the extraordinary benefits of compounding interest. KiwiSaver is an excellent example of compounding interest and is why it's such a fantastic thing.

How long will it take to double your money?
The rule of 72 states that if you divide the number 72 by an investment's annual rate of return after tax (i.e. the net return), you will get the number of years it will take for the investment to double in value. For example, if you stash $5,000 in an investment that returns 6% annually, your $5,000 will turn into $10,000 in 12 years (72 ÷ 6). Or, if you put the $5,000 in an investment that returns 12% annually, it will be worth $10,000 in just six years (72 ÷ 12).

PASSIVE VERSUS ACTIVE INVESTING

Before deciding which investment strategy or options might best suit you, I think it's worthwhile to understand how involved you want to be.

Passive investing

Passive investors, which accounts for most people, are not interested in putting a lot of time and effort into their investing. This could be for a range of reasons: it's the wrong time of life, they're busy with career and family, they already have an investment portfolio built up, they have a low risk profile, they are fortunate enough to be expecting a large inheritance, or they have investments, such as bank deposits, that don't need any management. Or perhaps investing simply does not ring their bells!

If you're a passive investor, you'll most likely have an expert managing your investments. It could be the fund manager or KiwiSaver provider, a financial planner or stockbroker managing your portfolio, or a property investment mentor. Once you have set up your investments, the management of them is passive for you. That doesn't mean that you don't pay any attention to them, though; you still need to keep an eye on your investments and review them on a regular basis and be in communication with your professional advisors.

If you want to be a passive investor, the earlier you start investing, no matter how small the amount is, the better off you will be. This is due to the effect of time on your investment value. If you want the value of your investments to grow, invest the interest or dividends you receive back into the investment. Ideally you should use the interest only once you reach the point when you have grown your investments and now need for them to provide you with an income (such as in retirement).

My theory is that passive investors should focus on

diversification, which means you have a number of ways you grow your wealth — such as manage your money smartly, pay off your mortgage faster, ensure you are in KiwiSaver, maybe have a small savings plan, or buy an investment property. Diversifying is a good strategy if you generally are less aggressive (and more risk averse), have less knowledge or interest in investing, or just want to spread your risk.

Active investing

The really grunty part of investing is for people who want to fast-track their wealth creation and are prepared to put in the time and effort. Active investing takes a lot more time, knowledge, skill and risk than passive investing. An active investor might spend more than 10 hours every week managing their investments. It might even be their full-time job. They are really focused on building their wealth and they often want higher returns, perhaps over a shorter time frame, and therefore are prepared to take on more risk and be more actively involved.

Given what is involved, active investors tend to be really passionate about what they are doing. They love spending hours learning about their craft. They have a thirst for knowledge, read a lot, attend seminars and courses, network, join investing groups and have a good team of professional advisors that they regularly liaise with. If you want to be an active investor, it is critical that learn your craft and hone your skills. This investment in your knowledge will lower your risk and increase your chances of success.

LEVERAGE

When I am working with my clients, I assess what resources they have to work with. I want to understand whether they have any initial capital to invest, how much spare income they have that they are comfortable adding on a regular basis, what their knowledge is, how much time they have and how involved they want to be, and if they have any particular skills or contacts that can be leveraged.

Leverage can be an important component of growing your wealth, particularly for active investors. Generally, leverage is the use of debt (borrowed capital) to undertake an investment or project. The result is to multiply the potential returns from a project. At the same time, leverage will also multiply the potential downside risk in case the investment does not pan out. It can also be about influencing something to get more power or value out of it.

I think of leverage in three main ways, as follows.

Money

Most of us have a pretty good understanding of leveraging money. In simple terms, it is using equity as security to borrow money. Some people refer to it as OPM — other people's money. Property investors in particular are very familiar with this, but so, too, are you if you are a homeowner. Usually, you put a deposit down and borrow funds to buy a property. If you didn't leverage your deposit to borrow, you would have to save the entire cost of the property. Property investors often borrow against the equity in their homes to buy an investment property. You can also leverage (borrow) against your business if a lending institution perceives there is value in it, and you can leverage against other assets, such as shares, although these options don't offer as much leverage as property, which is seen as more secure.

Time

No matter how wealthy you are, you can't buy time. This makes it one of the most valuable commodities of all. Not many people understand the power of leveraging time. Given it is a finite resource, you want to get the most out of how you spend your time as it can help you improve your finances.

As a property investor, for example, I am perfectly capable of doing some basic maintenance on my portfolio. In the past, for instance, I have painted a couple of properties. I can tidy the garden, mow the lawns and so on. Recently I learnt how to tile when we were renovating our home. Not a particularly good use of my time but for the most part I'm glad I did it as I learnt a lot — never again though! This is because I have a business and can earn more per hour than what I pay per hour for someone to do the maintenance work for me. If I had plenty of time, maybe it would be different.

As a business owner, I am aware that I have limited hours in my day, and I want to ensure that the tasks I perform deliver the best financial results. For most business owners there is always a never-ending list of tasks. Some of them deliver better value than others. Successful business people tend to be very good at prioritising activities according to which delivers the best leverage on their time.

Another example might be that you get a cleaner to do your housework and instead use the time to become better at managing your money. The point is that time is very valuable so use it wisely.

Unique ability

This is the area that I feel people understand the least. What is unique about you? There are a few things to consider:

- What are your innate abilities? These are traits that you were born with and generally come easily to you, or just as importantly don't. The best way to figure this out is to either do one or a number of the personality profile tests that are available, many of which are free online. Think about the things that are easy for you, that give you energy, rather than suck it out of you. I am good at creating things and setting up systems to make things efficient. After they are developed, I want someone else to run them as I get bored. Knowing this has made my life a lot easier. I can do detail if I focus on it, but in general it tends to make me quite tired, and I really need to pick when I do it.

- What are your particular skills? This is about your learned behaviour. What skills and knowledge have you developed in your life? A good example is tradespeople who are property investors. They can either do some of the work themselves if it makes sense from a time perspective or, given their knowledge, they could manage other tradespeople well. Another example could be you have good project-management skills or are great with numbers and managing money.

- Do you have any relationships to leverage? Maybe your partner is an accountant or your dad or cousin is a plumber. Who do you know that can help? It could also be that you are great at managing relationships. This is an area I have been successful with. I always think about how I can help others, and I cultivate and value relationships. As a result, I know a lot of people that are experts in their fields who can help me when I need it.

It is important not to focus on your weaknesses to bring them up to scratch; instead focus on the strengths and leverage those, as your results will be better. I don't beat myself up if I'm lousy at something; rather, I acknowledge it's not my strength, then find someone else to do it for me. Find others to work with that complement you. Choose an investment strategy that suits your abilities, and *do not* try to fit yourself into a strategy, which is what many people do. If you do find the right strategy to suit your innate abilities and skills and incorporate leverage into your thinking, you will do very well.

UNDERSTANDING RISK

Your risk profile is the degree of risk you are comfortable handling with your investments. What are you prepared to accept in pursuit of your investment objectives? Generally, the more risk you take with investments, the higher the potential return. Of course, most of us want the highest return possible on our investments but realistically are we prepared to take the risks associated with that? The investment world refers to conservative, balanced or moderate, and aggressive investors. These are terms many of us are aware of because of our KiwiSaver.

There is no such thing as a risk-free investment. Even if you invest your money into term deposits there is a real risk that over the long term your money will not keep pace with inflation and will devalue. If you are in your seventies this is far less of an issue than if you are in your thirties or forties. Shying away from all risk therefore comes with a risk in itself.

Risk is manageable but first you need to identify and quantify what the risks are. Here are the common ones.

Market risk

This is the risk of investments declining in value due to economic developments or other significant events that may affect the entire market. It includes **equity risk**, which applies to investment in shares. The market price of shares varies all the time with demand and supply. Equity risk is the risk of loss because of a drop in the market price of shares. **Interest rate**

risk affects debt investments such as bonds because of a change in the interest rate. For example, if the interest rate goes up, the market value of bonds will drop. **Currency risk** applies when you own foreign investments and is the risk of losing money due to a movement in the exchange rate. For example, if the NZ dollar becomes less valuable relative to the US dollar, your NZ shares will be worth less in NZ dollars.

Liquidity risk

The risk of being unable to sell your investment and get your money out when you want to, at a fair price. To sell the investment, you may need to accept a lower price. Sometimes you may not be able to sell the investment and you may need to wait until the investment matures. This is a common issue with investment property, which has a much longer selling time than shares.

Concentration risk

The risk of loss because you have all your money in one type of investment. When you diversify your investments, you spread the risk, generally over different types of investments, industries or locations.

Credit risk

Credit risk applies to debt investments such as bonds. If the company or government that issued the bond gets into financial difficulties, they may not be able to pay the interest or repay the principal at maturity.

Reinvestment risk

The risk of loss from not reinvesting the income you earn on your investment. A common example is spending the interest from a term deposit or the dividends from shares rather than reinvesting those earnings. This is a risk if you want to grow your investment as opposed to getting an income from them when you retire.

Inflation risk

This is the risk of a loss in your purchasing power because the value of your investments does not keep up with inflation. Inflation erodes the purchasing power of money, and over time the same amount of money will buy fewer goods and services. Inflation risk is particularly a factor with lower-risk investments such as term deposits, cash management trusts and bonds. Shares offer some protection against inflation because most companies can increase their prices. Share prices should therefore rise in line with inflation. Similarly, landlords can increase rents over time.

Horizon risk

The risk that your investment or time horizon (the length of time you expect to hold an investment) may be shortened because of an unforeseen event, such as losing your job or having an accident. This may force you to sell investments that you were expecting to hold for the long term. If you have to sell at a time when the markets are down, you may lose money.

Longevity risk

This is the risk of outliving your savings which, naturally, is most relevant for those who are retired or are nearing retirement.

Fee risk

This is not generally a risk that comes up when talking about investing, but I think it's an important one. In New Zealand we are a nation of DIYers and as a result we want to do everything ourselves and don't want to pay for good advice. I regularly see comments on social media about people changing to low-fee investments to save money. This can be a false economy as often some of the best-performing investments have the highest fees. I personally never consider fees on an investment, only net returns, which are after fees have been deducted.

All of these risks are relative to your personal circumstances, for example:

- If you are just starting out, you may have all your money in one investment and it's not practical to diversify.
- If you have lots of time, you can take on more risk as markets average out over time.
- If you are closer to the end of your life than the beginning, lower risk and more diversification is really important.
- If you are young and earn well, you could take on more speculative and high-risk investments such as crypto.
- If you are an active investor, you may want to put all of your focus into one investment type.

Investment options

KIWISAVER

Launched on 1 July 2007, KiwiSaver is a voluntary, work-based savings plan run by the government and the Inland Revenue Department (IRD). It is predominantly designed to help you save for your retirement. As of July 2022, there were 3.2 million members. KiwiSaver can be used to help towards the deposit of your first home (see Chapter 6). Here is an overview:

- You can choose to contribute 3%, 4%, 6%, 8% or 10% of your gross (before tax) wage or salary to your KiwiSaver account. It will be automatically deducted from your pay. You can change between rates at any time.
- Employers are required to contribute close to 3% of your gross salary if you contribute, unless your pay is grossed up, meaning that you get an extra 3% in your wages as opposed to it going into your KiwiSaver.
- You can still contribute if you are self-employed or don't work.
- At the time of writing, there's an annual government contribution that gives you 50% of each dollar you contribute up to a maximum of $1,042.86, even if you're not an employee, until you are 65.
- Your savings are invested on your behalf by the KiwiSaver provider of your choice. If you don't choose a provider, Inland Revenue will assign you to a default KiwiSaver fund. These providers are essentially a holding pen until you can decide which fund to choose.
- If you intend to apply for the government's First Home grant for your first home, you will need to contribute at least 3% of the adult minimum wage (based on a 40-hour week) or, if you are on a benefit, 3% of your annual benefit.
- The investment returns earned will automatically be reinvested into the fund, so your money grows over time.
- You can make voluntary contributions — lump sums or regular automatic payments — at any time, either directly to your KiwiSaver provider or through Inland Revenue.

Choosing your KiwiSaver scheme

All KiwiSaver schemes are registered with the government and managed by KiwiSaver providers. As with other investments like shares, property and even term deposits, KiwiSaver investments are not guaranteed by the government, although all schemes are tightly regulated. You can choose which scheme to join from a range of providers and you can change your scheme at any time, but you can only belong to one KiwiSaver scheme at a time.

Accessing KiwiSaver

In most cases you cannot access your KiwiSaver funds until you are 65 or have been in the scheme for five years, whichever is the later date. At 65 you can continue to contribute (although the government won't) and you will have a choice to take your funds as a lump sum or get regular withdrawals. There are some special circumstances allowing access:

- You may make a one-off withdrawal to help you buy your first home, after you have been with KiwiSaver for three years.
- Withdrawals may be permitted in cases of significant financial hardship, matrimonial separation, or serious illness.
- You can withdraw your money if you move permanently overseas, after having contributed to KiwiSaver for 12 months or more.
- KiwiSaver becomes part of your estate if you pass away.

For most people your KiwiSaver will be one of the biggest contributors to a financially secure retirement. However, few review their KiwiSaver regularly and have a set-and-forget strategy. This can be very costly. Being in the right fund can make a significant difference, especially when you factor in time. The difference between a conservative and growth fund is shown in the graph below.

KiwiSaver fund types compared

Conservative $184,000

Balanced $269,000

Growth $408,000

Assumptions: 30-year-old employee contributing 3% of $70,000 pre-tax salary, employer contributing 3%, and current balance $30,000.

Source: www.nationalcapital.co.nz

It is vital to make a proactive decision on which KiwiSaver fund to be in and to review it regularly. I highly recommend www.nationalcapital.co.nz who research all the providers and will review your KiwiSaver to ensure you are in the best fund for your objectives. There is no cost to you as the service is paid for by the KiwiSaver providers. There is also a ton of educational information on the website.

I am a bit biased as I am a director of and shareholder in this company. We loved it so much we bought it. But, seriously, the service is well worth a wee bit of your time.

THE SHAREMARKET

Shares (equities) have been shown to be the best long-term investment, surpassing property, cash and fixed interest as a generator of wealth. Any long-term indices (which track the value of prices) will show this, although you should note that they don't include the value of any leverage that could be used. This is why property investors always think that property is a better-performing asset class. Leverage can make a significant difference to an asset's returns on both the positive and negative side. There are several reasons why investing in shares is a good strategy for saving over the long term.

Flexibility and liquidity

At any given time, there are usually buyers and sellers in the market for most major companies. As a result, you can buy and sell at your convenience. This aspect of shares, known as liquidity, is in stark contrast to property, which can be expensive and time-consuming to buy and sell. While shares can be sold with one quick phone call or one quick click on the internet, property can take months to sell.

Cost

Another benefit of shares is that buying and selling them is very cheap in comparison to an asset class such as, again, property. Technology has dramatically decreased the cost of making a share transaction and increased the ease with which you can do it.

Low capital requirements

You need only a very small amount of money — as little as a couple of hundred dollars — to get started and buy your first shares.

Simplicity

Information on your investment and the market is easy to obtain. You can track share prices in the newspapers, on the internet, or on smartphone apps. Public companies are also required by law to produce an annual report (which is sent to shareholders), disclosing their financial track records for the previous year.

PROPERTY INVESTMENT

There are many types of property that qualify as investments, ranging from residential buildings to commercial units (including retail, office and industrial) or even forestry plantations. There are also various methods of investing in property. You can invest directly, go through a listed property trust, or use a unit trust. Below I will cover the basics of investing directly into residential property. In this context I'm referring to direct property, because indirect property in a listed property trust is the same as shares. The main things to consider are as follows.

Leverage

One of the biggest benefits of investing in property is the ability to use leverage, which is much harder to do with shares. This allows you to buy a property with a smaller deposit or use equity you have in other assets to secure your borrowing against. You get the full return (positive or negative) against the value of the property and not the cash you put in.

Cost

You need to be in a good financial position to be able to invest in property as opposed to shares when you can invest with only a few dollars. This may mean it will take you longer to be able to start.

Liquidity and time frame

Property is generally a long-term investment, 10 years plus, and is not very liquid. It can take months to sell a property, especially if the market is quiet. If you do need to sell quickly, you may need to drop your price a lot and therefore can lose money. You can trade (buy and sell property), but you really need to know what you are doing.

Adding value

Another key benefit of property is that you can add value to your property. If you want to be actively involved you can purchase an older property and renovate, add a minor dwelling on the site, add an extra room, or subdivide and build. There are lots of options to add value. You can't do this with the sharemarket.

SPECIALTIES

Specialty investments are quite specific and often high-risk investments. If they do well, you can make very high returns, but you can often lose a chunk of your money or in some cases all of it. Generally, you would only invest in these types of investments if you were comfortable losing what you have invested, and or have very specialist knowledge. Examples of these types of investments are gold, art and collectables, and — the most popular today — cryptocurrency. In most cases these types of investments should be only a small portion of your investment capital. If you are young with a good income, you could take on more risk and focus more on this type of investment.

There is a plethora of investment options available. Consider the options based on your individual circumstances and not what your friends are doing. Work out what your objectives are, do your research and, if possible, get professional advice.

The secrets of smart investing

Sorry to disappoint you, but I don't believe there are any real secrets to investing. Every year, though, millions of people around the world buy books and CDs, attend webinars, seminars and the like on a quest to find them. In fact, the secrets to investing are quite simply a number of basic principles.

BASIC PRINCIPLES

1. Start early

I cannot begin to stress how important it is to start as soon as possible. If I had a dollar for every time someone said to me that they wished they'd begun saving earlier, I would have a very big pile of money. Ideally you should work towards saving a minimum of 10% of your income over your entire working life. This is a principle of a world-famous book, *The Richest Man in Babylon* (1926) by George Clason.

When you are younger, your savings could be part of your KiwiSaver contribution, or it could be saving for a home deposit. While starting early is very valuable, it is never too late; just decide to begin today, no matter how little you are starting with.

2. Pay yourself first

Most of us spend what we have. A good principle is to transfer part of what you earn directly into your savings or investment account as soon as you get paid. The saying 'out of sight, out of mind' rings very true. One could argue that the reason most countries have a pension scheme is because the government figured out a long time ago that people can't budget.

3. Time in the market, not timing

Think long term. Far too many people try unsuccessfully to time the market. Don't wait for the *best* time to invest. The common saying, which is very true, is '*Time in the market, not timing*'. Markets can be quite unpredictable and volatile, particularly in the short term. Even the most experienced experts struggle to get their timing right. Typically, they work on a philosophy whereby as long as they get it right more times than they get it wrong, they are doing okay. This doesn't give the average person much hope of being successful with their timing. Focus on the long term and don't try to time the market.

4. Invest, don't gamble

To invest in something, you usually have a reasonable idea, based on factual information, that you will get a return over a period of time. Gambling, or speculating, can be very risky and usually requires a lot more skill and expertise; it's not for the average person. Let's look at some examples.

- *Investing* — you buy a managed fund of New Zealand companies, run by a known investment company.
- *Gambling* — you buy shares in an oil company based in Argentina because you have heard that there is an oil shortage, and the prices of these shares are going to dramatically increase.
- *Investing* — you buy a rental property in a city or large town where you know there is good demand for rentals, you have worked out the cashflow and are prepared to hold it long term so it will increase in value.
- *Gambling* — you buy a property off the plans in a brand-new resort; the real estate agent tells you the area is going to boom, and your plan is to sell quickly and make a profit. (Note: the gain on this activity is taxable.)

Gambling or speculating can be okay, provided you accept the risks associated with it. There are often higher returns, but there is also more potential to lose money. Some people might put, say, 10% of their investing money into something that is more of a high-risk gamble. This would be an amount that they could afford to lose if the investment went pear-shaped.

5. Have an investment strategy that suits your risk appetite

Everyone has a different attitude to risk. In my experience, approximately 80% of people fall into the average risk category. They can accept a certain amount of risk and can cope if their investments drop occasionally in value, as long as it's not too great a drop for too long. They don't necessarily expect huge returns; rather, they want a more consistently safe strategy.

It's important to know how you feel about risk. People become more accepting of risk when markets are strong, invest aggressively and forget about the potential downsides. When markets are weak, they suddenly find that they are far more risk averse. If you can't sleep at night when your shares drop even slightly in value, you shouldn't invest in them. If you can't deal with tenants trashing your property or not paying their rent (it's bound to happen at some point), don't buy an investment property. If you can sleep at night owing lots of money (investment debt), building an investment portfolio may suit you. If you are a conservative investor, stay away from private equity investments.

6. If it sounds too good to be true, it probably is!

Stay away from get-rich-quick schemes. The number of people who get caught up in scams is quite astonishing. I don't know if you get as many emails as I do for pleas from a minor royal in a foreign land promising you extraordinary amounts of money for your help getting their funds out of their country. You may laugh, but many people have had their fingers burnt believing such promises. (After all, why would they spend so much time on their emails if it didn't work?) Another common scam often targets high-earning professionals: you get a call from a 'stockbroker', based overseas, offering some fantastic share whose price is about to go through the roof, but for this 'opportunity of a lifetime' you must invest immediately before it's too late. If it sounds too good to be true, it probably is.

7. Keep it simple

Keep your investment strategy as simple as possible. The more complex it is, the harder you will find it to understand and therefore manage. A key component of successfully building a savings or investment fund is to keep doing it consistently over a long period. If you find it takes too much time to manage your investments, you won't do it. If you find it too hard to understand, you will also keep putting it off. Keep it simple and keep at it.

8. Be patient

It takes time. When talking to clients about building an investment portfolio, I encourage them to think at least 10 years ahead. Almost all investments have cycles. Typically, they go up, may go sideways for a while, and may go down before they eventually go up again. Over the long term, investments should go up in value. Ten years should smooth out the effects of market cycles.

9. Don't overreact to short-term fluctuations

Research indicates that the people who invest for the long term have received higher returns than those who invest short term or try to time the market. This is simply because investors tend to buy when the market is high (when everyone is talking about a great investment) and sell when the market is low or not performing well (when everyone is talking about what a lousy investment it is). When an investment goes down in value, take a deep breath and ask yourself why you purchased that investment in the first place. If that reason is still there, hold on to it and ride through what tends to be, in most cases, a short-term fluctuation. It may even be a good idea to continue buying at 'sale' prices.

10. Always reinvest the interest

Always, always, always reinvest any income you receive from your investments (unless of course you are in retirement and living off the interest). If you invest $10,000 and spend the income from that $10,000, your investment will always be $10,000. This is a problem because of inflation which, over time, erodes the value of your $10,000. This means that in, say, 10 years' time, your $10,000 will buy much less than it does today. You want to ensure that, over time, the growth of your investment outpaces inflation.

11. Tax is not the main reason to invest

Please don't invest in something just because you feel that you are paying too much tax and you want to get some back. To get a tax rebate from the IRD, you must first have a loss. And much to some people's amazement, you only get back part of what you've lost. For example: if you made a loss of $6,000 and your personal tax rate was 33%, you will only get $2,000 back. Note: this doesn't apply to managed funds in respect of your personal tax return, and due to recent tax changes, any loss made from a property investment can only be offset against future profits. Losing a dollar to get a third back is a lousy reason for making an investment. Depending on the circumstances, however, it can be a bonus. When accountants tell people to buy an investment property, or business owners to buy new cars, because they are paying too much tax, it drives me nuts. Isn't it about making money? Surely you would be happy to have a huge tax bill, as it would mean you've made lots of money!

12. *Keep your emotion out of your investing*
- I liked the look of the property so I thought it would be a good investment.
- I really like the CEO of XYZ Ltd or like their products, so I bought their shares.
- I'll just wait until they get back up to $5 again before I sell my shares. (What happens if it takes 25 years?)
- My neighbour who I was chatting to over the fence said they were a good buy.
- Everyone else seems to be buying them, so maybe I should.

Do these sound familiar? Do you think they are solid reasons to buy an investment or are they based on emotion? Emotion plays a big part in the way people invest. Successful investors learn to invest on the numbers and facts, not emotions.

13. *Work with an expert or become one yourself*
If from a very early age you can start putting 10% of your income into a long-term savings plan, you will develop a reasonable sum of money for retirement. If you leave it much later, you will likely need some help and will need to save a higher amount. Far too many people take advice from their friends and family about investments, which I believe can be a case of the *blind leading the blind*. In New Zealand today, approximately half of all adults have either negative net worth or, by the time they cash up, almost no net worth. Throw in the fact that for most New Zealanders the government Superannuation is their only source of income in retirement, and you must wonder if friends and family give good advice! Ask yourself if the person you seek advice from is qualified to give that advice. If the answer's no, you need to talk to or learn to become an expert or seek professional advice.

14. Get advice

I would expect most financially successful people would be getting some form of professional advice and the more successful they are, the more advice they probably get. There is a lesson in that!

> *'The two best times to start saving are ten years ago and today.'*
> —ANON.

Case Study: Investing for the long term (Peter — Auckland)

I was lucky enough to join the workforce in the 1980s when house prices weren't such an eye-watering multiple of average incomes. Still, scratching together enough for a deposit for my first home wasn't easy and meant forgoing luxuries and the big OE. My purchase was a very basic flat but, at 25, at least I was on the property ladder. I've always been conscious of debt and not letting it get out of hand. As a result, I have avoided mistakes like extending the mortgage for a new car or overseas holiday. There are some simple rules I've always lived by:

1. Apart from buying property, if I can't pay for it in cash, I can't afford it
2. The only debt I'll have is a mortgage, and
3. Repay the mortgage as quickly as possible. It feels so much better when mortgage payments are more loan repayment rather than interest!

I was also lucky to work for an employer in my twenties and thirties that provided a staff superannuation scheme. When I finally resigned to work elsewhere, it provided a nice start for my future investment portfolio. I would periodically add lump sums when I received bonuses, avoiding the temptation to splurge. That was no easy thing. Through the last couple of decades, I have witnessed the marvels of compounding returns and investment earnings that now comfortably outweigh the amount contributed. KiwiSaver is also a no-brainer when your employer and the government contribute.

I haven't made too many mistakes on the way other than learning I'm hopeless at timing markets. I have always adopted a long view of investment strategy because, in my opinion, better long-term returns trump short-term volatility every time. That said, the Global Financial Crisis provided some nervous moments and, even now, it's not fun watching markets fall. Which leads to another rule. Don't keep looking at your portfolio or KiwiSaver investments when markets are falling.

Finally, being debt free and having meaningful investments provides a wealth of financial freedom and choices.

In a Nutshell
- KiwiSaver will become one of your biggest financial assets so pay attention to it and ensure you are in the right fund.
- Saving is more for the short term while investing is more for the long term and to fund your semi or full retirement.
- Always align your saving and investing with your goals.
- Time is your best friend so the sooner you start the better.
- Education and advice will help accelerate your wealth — get both.

Buy a home

BUYING A HOME is one of the biggest financial decisions you will make in your lifetime. However, in the last 40 years or so in New Zealand, home ownership has steadily declined from around 75% to approximately 64%. Statistically speaking that is quite a significant drop. Today we live in a more transient society. People move around a lot more with their jobs, are getting married later, want more flexibility with their living arrangements, and home ownership just doesn't seem important for some. Sadly, many view owning a home as no longer within their reach due to it being increasingly difficult to save for a deposit and afford the mortgage repayments, especially in the major cities and more highly desirable and expensive areas.

Why buy?

Home affordability gets a lot of airtime and rightly so. Everyone should have the ability to buy a home if they choose. There is no doubt that housing is expensive in New Zealand, but is it as bad as some people think? Is this constant exposure to affordability challenges creating a false reality? Or is it simply the numbers are bigger due to time and inflation? For instance, about 40 years ago in my early teens one of my first jobs paid me $1.99 per hour, while in 2022 for a young person over 16 years old the minimum starting-out or training hourly rate is $16.96. About 30 years ago I purchased my first home in one of the worst suburbs in Palmerston North for $87,000. I lived in it for a short time before renting it out and eventually sold it only a few years ago for $360,000. I worked pretty much two full-time jobs and lived off the smell of an oily rag to save for the deposit. My dad helped me tidy it up and paint it and all my furniture was either free (from old things friends and family didn't want) or second hand. My first home was small and basic and not in a great area, but it was all I could afford at the time, and I saved pretty much all I earnt above the absolute necessities to get the deposit. I truly believe you can still do this in today's environment if you are focused and work hard enough.

Regardless of what house prices are today, they are what they are, so we just need to make the best of them. Given it can be tough to get your first home, why bother? Here is why I am very pro buying a home:

- There is a sense of pride in owning a home.
- You can do with it what you want; for instance, redecorate it to your own sense of style.
- It gives you a sense of stability and security. You won't have the risk of a landlord giving you notice to leave.
- Paying off the mortgage is a great form of compulsory savings and builds your overall wealth.
- You have a reasonable amount of predictability in what it will cost you over time, other than there will be short-term fluctuations in mortgage interest rates.

- Most importantly, one day you won't have a mortgage and it will be yours with nothing to pay other than maintenance, rates and insurance.

Why not rent instead?

In the long term, buying is cheaper than renting. Initially your mortgage payments may be more than what you would pay in rent. However, you will spend less over the life of the loan if you buy. Rents will rise over time and most likely become more than your mortgage payments. When you factor in the probability that property values go up over the years, owning a home makes even more sense. The best thing is that when your mortgage is paid off you have no more payments and you own your home outright.

EXAMPLE: BUYING VS RENTING

Let's look at an example.

Buying a home

Let's say you purchase a home for $700,000 with a deposit of $140,000 and pay off a principal and interest mortgage of $560,000 over 25 years. Your monthly repayments would be $3,274, assuming an average interest rate over that period of 5%. If the average long-term capital growth rate is 5%, your home will be worth $2,436,903 in 25 years.

Now, before you fall off your chair, note that we are talking 25 years, and that inflation will account for approximately half of this increase in value (assuming inflation averages 2.5% over the long term).

Saving and renting

Now let's look at a renting scenario. To be in roughly the same position financially as you would if you bought a home, you would need to pay your weekly rent *and* save $4,000 each month for 25 years (starting with no savings). This will give you $2,405,889. Or starting with $140,000 (the same amount as for your house deposit) you would need to pay your rent *and* save $3,200 per month to give you a total value at the end of 25 years of approximately $2,400,952. Examples assume 5% annual after-tax growth and that you will make every single payment over those 25 years.

In the vast majority of cases, you will be better off financially buying a home than saving and renting. It is also important to note that very few people have the discipline to save consistently like this over the long term, therefore making it much more likely that you will be better off buying a house and paying down the mortgage.

Saving for a house deposit

Saving for a home deposit can be tough and it does take time, focus and discipline. Herein lies the challenge given we live in the 'need it now' society and we get tempted daily to buy stuff and spend our money. It's hard to have the resolve to say no and to save your money instead. I often hear how much harder it is today, but is that true? My father once told me that when he got married his boss shook his head and said he wondered how on earth as a young married couple they could afford to buy a house, given the prices were so high. Sound familiar? Interestingly, that was well over 50 years ago in Palmerston North.

HOW MUCH DO I NEED?

For a deposit, you want to be saving around 5–20% of the purchase price of the house you want to buy. As a first-home buyer you can sometimes borrow 90% instead of the normal 80% required by most lenders. The table below provides examples of how much you might need.

Purchase price	5%	10%	15%	20%
$500,000	25,000	50,000	75,000	100,000
$600,000	30,000	60,000	90,000	120,000
$700,000	35,000	70,000	105,000	140,000
$800,000	40,000	80,000	120,000	160,000
$900,000	45,000	90,000	135,000	180,000
$1,000,000	50,000	100,000	150,000	200,000

Ideally you would want to save as much as you can for a number of reasons. First, to make it easier to borrow. The more you have as a deposit, the lower the risk to the bank, who will be more likely to lend you money. Second, the higher the deposit, the lower the mortgage and the easier the repayments will be. Remember you have these repayments for many years so you don't want to feel too constrained by them. Also, if you have a low deposit you may have to pay a mortgage lenders insurance premium — sometimes called low-equity premium (see page 147).

USING YOUR KIWISAVER TO TOP UP YOUR DEPOSIT

KiwiSaver can be a great help with buying your first home and for some people it can make up most of their deposit. You don't want to be in a situation where you are in an aggressive fund and the market drops when you are ready to buy or discover that you are not eligible for as much as you thought. It is important to get advice as early as possibly to ensure you are maximising the potential benefits. The criteria are:

- You have been saving into your KiwiSaver for at least three years.
- You are intending to live in the property (KiwiSaver cannot be used to buy an investment property).
- You leave a minimum balance of $1,000 in your KiwiSaver account.
- If you currently own land, a home, or have a share in a property, you won't be eligible. However, if you have already owned a home, you may still be eligible if you are deemed to be in the same financial position as a first-home buyer.
- If you have a superannuation fund which is not KiwiSaver but is an equivalent, you may be able to use that.
- The property can only be in New Zealand

To apply for the withdrawal, contact your KiwiSaver scheme provider or relevant complying fund manager; if approved, payments will be made to your lawyer on or before settlement day.

KiwiSaver First Home Grant

If you've been contributing to your KiwiSaver for at least three years and contributing 3% of your income you may be eligible for a First Home Grant of up to $10,000 to top up your deposit. This is for each person so you could get up to $20,000 for a couple. The current criteria is:

- If you buy an existing home, you can get $1,000 for each of the three (or more) years you've paid into the scheme. The most you can get is $5,000 for five or more years.

- If you buy a new home or land to build on, you can get $2,000 for each of the three (or more) years you've paid into the scheme. The most you can get is $10,000 for five or more years.
- You have earned less than $95,000 before tax in the last 12 months, or less than $150,000 combined if one buyer with one or more dependants or two buyers. Note that these income levels may increase over time so check the latest details.
- You need to make a minimum deposit of 10% (including the money you can withdraw from your KiwiSaver).
- The purchase price of the property is within the regional house price caps which change so check at the time you are looking at buying.

To apply online for the First Home Grant, or simply find out more, visit Kāinga Ora at https://kaingaora.govt.nz/home-ownership/first-home-grant/

Family gift

The 'Bank of Mum and Dad' is now one of the biggest contributors of funds for first-home buyers. They could help with your deposit which could be gifted, or you might come to an agreement to pay it back later. It is essential that you get legal advice, so everyone is very clear on the expectations. If you have agreed to pay back the deposit later, it could affect your loan depending on when you've agreed to pay it back so check with your lender.

Often parents are lending their kids part of their retirement savings. In my experience the kids do not realise how significant this is. It's not such an issue if your parents are very well off financially, but that is not often the case. It may mean that

144 | GOOD WITH **MONEY**

parents need to work a number of years longer before they retire, or they have less to retire on, which may limit their lifestyle. Parents always want to help their kids and often put their needs first so while this can be a good option, make sure you understand what this may mean for your parents as well as yourself.

A guarantee from family

Another option instead of having the deposit gifted is for family to act as your guarantor. This is where you use the equity from your family's property as security for your loan. If they are choosing to act as your guarantor, they'll be responsible for some or all of your entire loan if you're not able to pay it. Again, it is essential that you get legal advice as there can be serious implications if you don't meet your loan obligations.

Mortgages demystified

Along with saving for your deposit it's important to put some thought into your mortgage, given it's likely to be your largest expenditure in life. It's not just a matter of rocking up to the bank and asking for a loan. Before you approach a lender, there are things to think about to be sure of getting the best mortgage for you.

HOW MUCH CAN YOU BORROW?

The amount you can borrow partly comes down to two things: how much a lender (usually a bank) will give you, and how much you think you can afford. It is really important that you work out what is realistic and comfortable for you. Don't overcommit yourself or you will be living on baked beans! Having said that, in today's regulated environment it is harder to get finance and you are far less likely to be able to over-borrow. Lenders are strictly guided by the Credit Contracts and Consumer Finance Act (CCCFA) which aims to protect vulnerable consumers from predatory lending practices. They must ensure they are only providing credit to people who can afford it. Additionally, the Responsible Lending Code ensures lenders act responsibly towards clients. Lenders will consider your overall financial position when deciding how much they will lend you and they require you to provide a lot of documentation to support it. It can take some time to prepare all of this so make sure you give yourself plenty of time to get a loan approval. They will consider:

Your deposit

Where is your deposit coming from? Is it coming from an existing property, cash/savings, your KiwiSaver account for first-home buyers, or a gift? You will need to provide proof of how you got your deposit. Having a good record of saving for your deposit is a good demonstration of how you manage your money.

Security

A lender looks to see how much you are borrowing in relation to how much equity you have, and uses a ratio called the loan-to-value ratio (LVR).

To calculate the LVR, divide the value of the loan by the value of the property.

The LVR on a $700,000 property with a loan of $560,000 is $560,000 \div 700,000 = 0.8 = 80\%$

Historically, LVR rules have generally been based on approximately 20% deposit to 80% borrowings. The deposit gives the lender a buffer in case you can't manage the loan and you need to sell the property. Lenders may lend you more than this if it is your first home, you have a good financial track record and you have enough income. It can be different again if you are buying an investment property, where currently the LVR is 40% for existing properties and 20% for new builds.

The LVR is worked out on the total value of all of your properties and loans. This means that you can borrow 100% on a property if you use another property or asset as security, as is often the case with investment properties.

Serviceability

This is about your income and expenses and how easily you can manage the loan repayments. The Debt Servicing Ratio (DSR) is used, which measures your cashflow to determine how easily you can manage the loan repayments. The DSR is the loan payments divided by the eligible income. Lenders generally allow 30–35% of your own income and 75–80% of your rental income as eligible income. This essentially means they don't want your repayments to take up more than 30–35% of your income.

Account conduct

Lenders look very carefully at your spending history and what you spend your money on. What are the financial commitments that you have, are you going to the casino every Friday night, how much are you saving . . .? They will check the activity on your recent bank statements and make sure it matches up with what you have told them on your loan application. They don't like free spenders. They will also look at your credit card balances and limits. Depending on how well you manage your money you may have to pay particular attention to your spending at least three months before you want to take out a loan.

Character

Your personal character will be another thing that can be considered. Are you a dependable person to lend money to? Do they see you as responsible with money or are they concerned that you have no idea how to manage your money? They are equally concerned about you getting into trouble as they are getting their loan repaid.

Short-term debt

Clearing as much short-term or consumer debt as possible will strengthen your application. This may include reducing your credit card limits, as the banks consider your full limit as current borrowings even if you never use the full limit or pay off your balance each month.

Mortgage lenders insurance

This is also often called a low-equity premium and is what a lender (bank) will charge you if you borrow over 80% of the value of a property. The reason they charge it is because any borrowings over 80% increase the risk of the loan being able to be paid back. If you get into trouble and cannot make the payments, the 20% buffer on an 80% loan ensures that if the lender has to sell the property, they can be pretty certain of recouping all their money. If you are borrowing more than 80% of the house value, the low-equity premium is effectively their insurance. The fee is usually added to the amount borrowed so you can pay off the fee over the term of your mortgage.

TYPES OF MORTGAGES

Let's explore some of the terminology and different types of mortgages which can be daunting when you are starting out.

Principal and interest (P&I)

This is by far the most common type of loan for homeowners. It's when the *loan* repayment includes both the *principal* (amount of the money borrowed) as well as the *interest* accrued on that principal. In the early years your loan repayment mainly consists of interest. As the years go by the amount of interest you pay decreases while the amount of principal you pay increases. At the end of your loan term, you will own your home with no debt.

Mortgage repayments: principal and interest loan

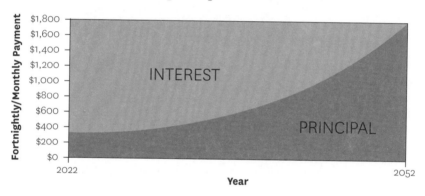

Interest only

This is when only the interest is paid. With the soaring cost of housing over recent years, I have seen more people taking out interest-only mortgages, and this is extremely concerning. You might be tempted to take this route because the repayments are lower and therefore more affordable. The danger is that you don't pay off the house and the amount of your mortgage will not decrease over time. Some people use an interest-only mortgage to get them through a 'tight spot', then change back to a principal and interest option when their finances improve. If this is your plan, it is crucial that you remember to do it as soon as you are able. Banks will only give you an interest-only loan for a short period — generally two to five years — as they do want you to pay down your loan. Interest-only loans are more common for property investors who also have their own home on which they are paying principal and interest. If it is your own home, do not have an interest-only mortgage unless absolutely necessary for a short period of time.

Mortgage repayments: interest-only loan

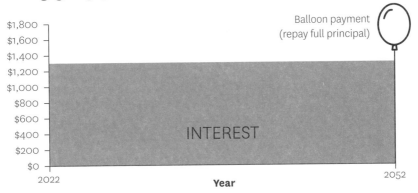

Fixed

A fixed mortgage is when the interest rate is set for a specific time frame, usually from six months to five years, the most common being one, two or three years. The advantage of a fixed rate is that you know exactly what your repayments will be over the term, which makes it easier to budget. The downside is that you can be limited in making extra payments if you want to pay off your mortgage faster.

Floating

A floating or variable mortgage is one where the interest rate on the loan goes up or down depending on what the market is doing. This means your repayments will increase or decrease if your lender changes their floating rates. In practical terms when interest rates rise, your repayments go up, and when the interest rates fall, your repayments follow suit. Although this can make budgeting trickier, these mortgages are more flexible if you want to increase your regular payments or pay off lump sums.

Revolving credit

Revolving-credit mortgages come in a number of variations and have different names, but basically they give you the structure of a regular principal repayment schedule with added benefits. You can pay off as much as you like or simply pay the interest each month, and you can reborrow up to your limit any time you like, giving you ongoing access to credit. Since interest is calculated daily and charged monthly, the lower your average daily loan balance is, the less interest you are charged.

These mortgages are a great tool for paying off your debt faster, but they are only for the very disciplined, as they effectively work like an overdraft. Some do have a reducing balance which does force you to pay off at least some principal over time. Unless you are disciplined, they may not be a good tool for you. They can be great for property investors.

Offset

In an offset mortgage, your savings are linked to your mortgage. Or, to put that another way, instead of earning interest on your savings, the money is offset against your mortgage. As a result, you pay less interest on that debt. For example, if you had a $500,000 mortgage and $30,000 in various bank accounts, you would only be charged interest on $470,000.

This mortgage allows you to save for holidays, renovations, emergency funds and so on in separate bank accounts (easier for your money management) and effectively lower the amount of mortgage you pay interest on, which is especially handy given you earn a much lower interest rate on your savings accounts. Essentially, the more money you have in your bank accounts, the less mortgage interest you have to pay. I really like offset mortgages, but only a few banks offer them.

LOAN TERM

Traditionally mortgages have been taken out for a 25-year term. Today, however, the default term is 30 years. If you are older, say 50, then a 20-year term is more likely. A longer term can be attractive because the regular monthly payments are lower. However, the total amount of interest you pay over the full term of the loan is much higher. For example, on a $560,000 mortgage at 5%, the total cost of the interest (not including repayment of the borrowed amount) is $422,556 for a 25-year term and $522,922 for a 30-year term. That's a whopping difference of $100,366! Ideally you want to pay your mortgage off as fast as you can and reduce the total amount of interest you pay.

> **Tip:** Work out what different interest rates will mean to your regular mortgage payments — look at 5%, 6% and 7% — and see if you are comfortable with the repayments at these levels.

WHY USE A MORTGAGE ADVISOR?

Rather than going directly to a lender yourself, consider using a mortgage advisor. These days it is very common to use one. They are professionals who are well trained and specialise in liaising between lenders and borrowers. All lenders are slightly different and may suit some situations more than others. Mortgage advisors will know which lender will suit your individual circumstances best. It is common to get one level of borrowing with one bank but get far more with another. Your mortgage advisor will manage this process and may go to more than one bank for you. They will help you set up the most effective loan structure, negotiate interest rates, facilitate special offers like cash-backs as well as just generally guiding you and giving you advice.

A mortgage advisor is paid by the bank or lender when a loan is taken out by you. Sometimes if a mortgage is complex and goes through a specialist lender, there is a fee for you to pay. This will apply to a very small proportion of mortgages, and the mortgage advisor must advise you at the time what that fee will be. Most advisors will add value to your mortgage dealings and should be available to help you in the long term — for instance, if you have any questions down the track, need to refinance at some point, or maybe get another loan. As with all professionals not all are created equal so do some homework before deciding who to use. Given using a mortgage advisor is a free, or mostly free service, why would you not use an expert?

Choosing a home

Gosh, this is a biggie! Having a great home makes such a difference to how you feel and live your life so there is much to consider. Here are some things to think about:

- What is your budget? Your lender or mortgage advisor will be able to tell you this. Be careful not to borrow so much that you have nothing left in your budget after your repayments.
- Have a look at how different interest levels affect your repayments. For example, current interest rates are around 5–6%, which is at the low end of what they have

been for a while. See if you can afford the repayments at
7–7.5%, which is where the average rates have been over
the longer term. You don't want to be in a situation where
you cannot afford your payments if interest rates rise.

- Helping Kiwis get into their first home is really important
  for the government, regardless of which party is in power,
  so do some research and see what help there is available.
  For example, KiwiBuild works with developers to provide
  affordable homes via a ballot system.
- Consider which area you want to live in. Is it close to work,
  close to family and friends, within the catchment of a good
  school, close to shops?
- What type of home do you want? Apartment, villa,
  townhouse, small or large section, old vs new? How many
  bedrooms, and how big a garage?
- Make a list of what you are looking for and divide it
  into three columns. Include the must-haves (i.e. the
  deal breakers), things that are important but you can
  compromise on, and the nice-to-haves but don't really
  matter. If you are a couple, it can be useful to create a list
  each and then compare them. This exercise helps you
  develop your shopping list as such. It's likely to change as
  you start looking, which is totally fine, but having it can
  stop you from making bad decisions.
- Now for the tough part! How does what you want stack up
  against what you can afford? Often there is a large chasm
  between the two and it is likely you may need to make
  some compromises.
- Do your market research. Work with real estate agents, but
  also do your own homework and get to know the market
  in the areas you are considering. When it comes to putting
  an offer in you will be well informed about the value and

hence the price you should be paying for the property.

- Get your lawyer involved before you finalise the sale and purchase agreement to ensure you have the correct conditions and clauses.
- Remember that your real estate agent is a salesperson and their primary duty (fiduciary duty) is to the person who pays their commission, which in most cases is the vendor, not the buyer. Some are very knowledgeable, but some have only been in real estate a short period of time and have limited expertise. If you have done your homework, you can be far more discerning.
- As part of your due diligence, get a valuation, LIM report (Land Information Memorandum — a council report on the property) and building inspection to make sure you know what you are buying. This is a costly exercise but will be even more costly if you purchase a property with issues. Getting these reports done should be conditions in your sale and purchase agreement. If you are going to auction, these will need to be completed beforehand. These days in most cases the bank will require a valuation as part of your finance and will have certain valuers they use. Check this out with your mortgage advisor and lender, otherwise you could end up having to get two valuations.
- Put some thought into the most suitable mortgage structure for your personal circumstances. Your lender or mortgage advisor can help you with this.
- Always do a thorough pre-settlement inspection a day or two before you settle to make sure that everything you thought was included as part of the sale and purchase agreement is still there. You might be surprised how often it's not. Run the taps, turn on the lights, open the garage door, check the chattels that are included. If there is a

problem, your lawyer can hold some settlement money back until the issues are resolved.

- If you are planning to renovate, do a detailed budget of the costs, double it (in my experience this is what I have typically seen) and see if you can afford it, and that the work will be worth it.

THE COSTS

On top of the quoted or likely house price comes a raft of other costs. These may seem small compared with the house price, but you do need to factor them into your budget. They include:

- legal conveyancing fees: $2,000–3,000, depending on the complexity of the mortgage
- bank loan administration fee: around $150 but varies. You can often negotiate not to pay this
- mortgage lenders insurance if you borrow more than 80%; this varies a lot depending on how much over 80% you borrow
- house valuation: $700–$1,000+ depending on the value of the house
- building inspection report: $500–$1,000
- LIM report: $150–$400, depending on the council and how quickly you need one done
- connection fees for the phone, internet, power, TV, etc.
- moving costs: approximately $120 per hour

In addition, on an ongoing basis you may need to allow for:

- house and contents insurance
- mortgage repayment insurance, to cover your repayment upon death or a major illness

- rates
- body corporate fees if the property is a unit title
- regular maintenance

Pay off your mortgage faster

Now you have your home or are close to it give some thought to how you pay off your mortgage. This is where your mortgage structure is important. I have worked with many clients over the years who have saved tens of thousands of dollars — some hundreds of thousands — by structuring their mortgages differently, being smarter with their money, and increasing their payments.

People tend to go into remote control and pay the standard minimum payments over a 25-year (or 30-year) term. It may be that you cannot afford more than the minimum at this time but if you can, paying off your mortgage faster is a fantastic way to get ahead financially. By accelerating your payments, you will guarantee that you can save thousands of dollars over the term of your loan. Most people don't realise the significant difference these additional payments make, regardless of how small they may be.

Most bank and mortgage advisor websites have simple calculators that you can use to work out how much your mortgage is costing you. Let's look at the example below if you borrow $500,000.

$500,000 mortgage	30 years	25 years	20 years	15 years
Interest rate	5%	5%	5%	5%
Monthly payment	$2,684	$2,922	$3,300	$3,954
Total interest paid	$466,894	$377,781	$292,181	$211,831

Here, I have assumed an interest rate of 5%. Look first at the 30-year column. With the monthly repayment of $2,684, the total amount of interest paid over that term is $466,894 — *and that's on top of the original $500,000 you borrowed!* And yes: it's *heaps* of interest!

Now let's move along to the 25-year column. You will see that if you increase your payments from $2,684 to $2,922 per month (an additional $238) you will save yourself $89,113 in interest over the period of your loan and you will be mortgage free five years earlier.

Moving along to the 20-year column, increasing your payments from $2,684 to $3,300 per month (an additional $616) you will save $174,713 in interest and you will be mortgage free 10 years earlier.

If you have quite a bit of extra income you can use, let's look at the 15-year column. Here, increasing your monthly payments from $2,684 to $3,954 (an additional $1,270) will save you $255,063 in total interest and you will have paid off your loan and be debt free in 15 years. Yes — that's 15 years earlier, not to mention 15 years of not paying $2,684 each month!

You can clearly see from this example what a big difference those extra payments make over a length of time. Don't underestimate the money you will save by doing this. Most people are not only astounded by the amounts, but they also suddenly develop a strong motivation to pay off their mortgage much faster. Even if all you can afford today is an extra $10 per week — just two lattes — the money you will save will be well worth it in the long run. Every year or when your fixed mortgages come up for renewal have a think about whether you can make extra payments. There are ways to make those extra payments with flexibility, meaning you are not committed to the higher payments if things become tight.

PAY FORTNIGHTLY INSTEAD OF MONTHLY

Another tip is to consider paying your mortgage fortnightly, rather than the standard monthly. If you make 26 fortnightly payments each year instead of 12 monthly ones, you essentially make an extra month of payments. This means you pay more principal over the course of the year, which means you pay your mortgage off faster and save interest. You will need to consider how this fits into your budget cycle; that is, whether you work on a weekly, fortnightly or monthly budget.

CONSIDER YOUR MORTGAGE STRUCTURE

Many people believe that getting the lowest interest rate is the most important thing to consider when getting a mortgage. This is not necessarily the case. For example, I have seen many people fix their entire mortgage for three years but who can afford a lot more than the minimum payments. There are often limitations and fees associated with any additional payments you make on a fixed loan. Often people have the best intentions of saving money into a separate bank account and making some lump-sum payments when the fixed rate expires, but usually the money gets spent elsewhere.

Consider instead having a combination of the fixed and floating mortgage or a fixed and revolving credit facility (if you are disciplined). Even if you are paying a slighter higher overall interest rate (floating rates can be higher than fixed rates), you can often save thousands of dollars over the long term because you end up paying off more of the principal.

Case Study: Becoming a property investor (Nic — Wellington)

I have been investing since 2011, mainly in investment property, although I also invest in shares, managed funds, crypto and peer-to-peer lending.

Property

The most important thing for my development as an investor has been to get as much expert advice and education as possible. I attended Property Apprentice in 2011 and since then I have bought a number of 'buy and hold' rental properties in Auckland, Tokoroa and Wellington. Being educated in property investment has meant I have the skills to access each part of the market. Even if I can't buy at that time, I am always planning ahead and looking for opportunities to grow my portfolio.

My biggest challenge is servicing my debt, so I make sure I am well versed on subjects like money, finance and business. I often use offset loans, to ensure I don't pay more interest than I need to. Buying well grows wealth but so does not paying more on fees than you have to. Every little angle counts.

Things that have helped me and been important in my investment journey:

Keeping positive

There are two ways to look at things: glass half empty or glass half full. It's important to keep reminding yourself that getting ahead financially isn't easy or else everyone would be doing it. Your mindset, seeing the positive and thinking outside the square help you move forward during the tough times.

Have a plan, but be prepared to change it

'If you change the way you look at things, the things you look at change.' — WAYNE DYER.

There is nothing wrong with changing your plan, especially if you are facing a brick wall. I started out convinced that I was going to buy 10 properties in 10 years. At the time that was achievable. I was tracking pretty well towards my goal for the first four years — and then the market changed. There was no way I could buy any further properties in Auckland, and I thought that was the end of the road for me. I had been only looking in Auckland because that was what I had always done.

After some thought, I realised there were other ways to get back into the Auckland market if I just changed the way I looked at it. So I did! I bought a property in Tokoroa, in fact more than one. My property friends thought I had lost my mind, but I was in a position of doing nothing in Auckland or doing something somewhere else.

Find your why or whys

Dig deep to establish why you want to achieve your goals, and remind yourself of them regularly. It's what will keep you pushing through the tough times.

Service and freedom are two of my whys and, trust me, I think about them regularly, especially the freedom one!

My 'service why' is to provide warm, secure housing. Not just for those who can't afford to buy their own home but also for those who choose to do other things with their money.

Freedom for me means being able to do what I want, when I want. I still want to work in some capacity, but I want to work to my schedule. Whether it's work, committee work, being with friends, travelling or just walking my dog at the beach, if I gain more freedom I have more time for all my other whys.

So, what's yours? Dig deep for it, and don't be shy to change it when you need to.

In a Nutshell

- Buying your own home and paying it off is important for your financial future.
- Save for a home deposit in a separate account and put a goal around it.
- Chasing the lowest interest rate is not the only thing to consider when choosing the best mortgage.
- Using a mortgage advisor can help you get a better result.
- If you can pay off your mortgage faster than the standard 25- or 30-year term it can save you tens, even hundreds, of thousands of dollars over the long term.

Plan for the worst

Insurance is a means of protection from financial loss. It enables you, for a fee, to pass the risk of an event happening on to an insurance company.

NOT EVERYTHING IN LIFE goes according to plan and you just never know what will happen, so putting some contingencies in place to ensure you cover yourself if the unexpected happens is important. None of us like insurance, but it is an essential part of our lives. Generally, we are pretty comfortable insuring our property, car and household contents, but when it comes to insuring ourselves, we are more reluctant. If you are lucky, you might get through your life and never have to claim on insurance, but I would think the chances of that might be similar to winning the lotto!

The first line of defence for covering any risks life throws at you is your rainy-day or emergency fund, which I covered

in Chapter 2, or a revolving-credit facility covered in Chapter
6. If the unexpected happens most people will have a balance
of $10–20,000 in their emergency account (if they followed
the guideline of having enough to cover three to six months
of expenses put aside). Or you can have access to a revolving-
credit facility. However, these funds will be enough to cover only
smaller events.

If something major happens, unless you are in a very strong
financial position, you need to consider putting insurance cover
in place. Insurance is not something you can go out and buy when
you need it, as by then it is too late! Insurance is a necessary
evil: it's about planning for the 'what ifs' before they happen.
Understandably, few people look forward to having a conversation
with an insurance advisor as it will cost you money. I have been in
the financial services industry for almost 25 years now and have
seen many situations when having good insurance has been an
absolute godsend. There have also been situations where it has
broken my heart to see some of the tragedies that people have
experienced and the challenging and stressful financial positions
they have found themselves in due to having no insurance cover.

Please don't put your head in the sand. Even if you decide you
don't want any insurance, at least go through the process so you
understand what risks you wish to transfer (insure) and which you
are comfortable self-insuring (i.e. you live with the consequences).

Insurance overview

Our home, household contents or other belongings can be
expensive to buy. Often it is tough to be able to afford to repair
or replace these things if they are damaged or destroyed. By
paying a fee (premium) to an insurance company they will pay
the costs related to incidents covered by the policy.

FIRE AND GENERAL INSURANCE

Fire and general insurance is essentially asset insurance. It covers things rather than people. Below are the main types:

House insurance

- *Insured value* — pays a specific amount based on the market value of your home at the time you take out the policy. It is the cheapest option but is not often used as it may not cover the amount to rebuild your property, or take into account any increases in your property's value.
- *Replacement cover* — worked out on the square metre area of your property (the building and improvements) and will pay to rebuild your property regardless of the cost. This is the cover most people use.
- *Landlord's insurance* — designed specifically for rental properties. It covers issues such as loss of rent, malicious damage, damage from meth labs, and so on.

Contents insurance

This covers the contents of your house and other belongings while they are in your house or temporarily in another part of the country. In the event of loss, some items are paid out at their replacement value (cost to replace), while others are paid at their indemnity value (market value, i.e. if they were sold). Always itemise any expensive items like a camera or jewellery on your policy so you know they are covered.

This policy will also provide public liability insurance, which is particularly important if you are renting and you accidentally damage the house (or, worse, leave an iron on and the house burns down); this cover will pay the landlord's insurance cover to replace the home.

Car insurance

Next to your home your car may be one of the most expensive items you own and can be costly to replace or repair if it is stolen or damaged in an accident. Motor vehicle insurance will pay to repair or replace your car if these events occur. There are three types:

- *Third-party cover* — the most basic insurance and therefore the cheapest. It covers you for causing damage to someone else's car, but not to your own.
- *Third-party, fire and theft* — covers you for the above, and if it catches fire or is stolen (a good compromise if you can't afford comprehensive but, say, your car is crucial for your job).
- *Comprehensive cover* — the most common and covers any damage to your car and if you damage someone else's car.

The cost of car insurance will vary depending on your age (more expensive if you are under 25), claims history, any speeding tickets you have received, the level of excess you are prepared to take, and the make and type of vehicle.

PERSONAL INSURANCE

Personal insurance is not about what you own but rather insuring against any financial strain you and your family could face if your circumstances suddenly change. Here is an outline of the main types of personal insurance:

Medical insurance

With the constant rising costs of medical care and growing lengths of hospital waiting lists, this insurance gives you the fast track to private medical care. There are two main types of medical insurance: the most common is hospitalisation and

166 | GOOD WITH **MONEY**

specialist care, while comprehensive covers GP, dentist and optician visits and prescription costs.

> **CASE STUDY**
> **Tiare**, at 49, was a married father of two with a hectic lifestyle juggling family commitments and work as an engineer. Suddenly he suffered a heart attack, and everything changed. Not only did Tiare have to take some time off work and then really slow down, he also needed angioplasty — a procedure that would reopen his blocked blood vessels. He could wait for public treatment, or get it done privately — at a cost of around $20,000. As with most medical conditions, rapid treatment was key to a good outcome, so with his medical insurance policy he was able to have the procedure done privately almost immediately, helping him return to health faster and get back to work.

Consider:
- Is access to fully funded private healthcare important if a family member requires hospitalisation or surgery?
- Are you able to self-fund day-to-day treatment or medical costs (GP/prescriptions/dentist)?
- Would a claims excess be useful to reduce the cost of the insurance?

Income protection

Also known as disability income, income protection is an important type of insurance as it enables you to safeguard one of your most valuable assets: your livelihood or your income. For example, a 40-year-old earning $75,000 per annum after tax has a potential future income of $1.875 million (25 years × $75,000). It is the potential loss of this income that an income protection policy is insuring. A monthly sum is paid to you if you are not able to work due to illness or injury. Your policy will usually have a waiting period of four, eight or 13 weeks, chosen by you, before any income is paid, and payments will usually continue for a chosen period (usually to the age of 65).

There are two types of policy:

- Indemnity value — enables you to insure up to 75% of your gross taxable income. You advise the insurers of your annual salary/wage when you apply for the cover and must provide proof of earnings when you claim. A risk here is that if your income drops for a few years, you may end up paying for more cover than the payouts you receive in the event of a claim.
- Agreed value — suits self-employed individuals, or salaried employees where a large portion of their income is bonus- or commission-based. With this policy you provide proof (via previous years' taxation statements or payslips) of what your earning ability is, and the insurers will set in stone what they will pay out in the event of a claim.

CASE STUDY

At 39, **Varsha** had it all: a high-powered career as a human resources consultant and a young child she adored. She realised that as the sole income provider, she and her daughter needed some security in case she was unable to work. Just two years later, a mammogram revealed that Varsha had cancer. Through her income protection policy, she received a benefit of $5,200 a month. This enabled her to stop worrying about money and concentrate on getting well.

Consider:
- Might the extended disablement of the main income earners result in the loss of vital household income?
- If so, how long can you survive before your current income ceases and you need a top-up?
- How long will you need it for?

Trauma protection

Sometimes referred to as serious illness cover, trauma protection is a lump-sum payment, payable if you suffer a life-threatening illness, such as a heart attack, stroke, paralysis or cancer. Like life insurance and total and permanent disablement insurances (see below), this can be used to pay off any debts or provide an income you may need in the wake of a traumatic event. As this is one of the most expensive insurances you can buy, it is most used to cover unforeseen expenses such as the cost of medical treatment (including shortfalls in treatments not covered by health insurance), short-term income (cash buffer), rehabilitation requirements (including career retraining) and home help.

CASE STUDY

At 53 **John** had a great life. He had spent 15 years building up his very successful consultancy business. With his two children now grown up and independent, John and his wife were enjoying the freedom of being able to pack up and go sailing whenever they wished. But John then suffered a heart attack, which immediately confined him to bed and kept him off work — and the boat — for three months. Through his trauma protection cover, John was paid a lump sum of $100,000 immediately upon his diagnosis. This enabled him to clear his regular bills until his monthly income protection payments of $6,000 started after three months. With no financial stress, John could concentrate on getting well, and 12 months later he was back in business.

Consider:
- Would extra cash be helpful in getting you through a serious medical event such as cancer, heart attack or stroke?
- Would monthly mortgage and other liability obligations need to be met for a time or would debt reduction be needed?
- Do you have regular education commitments?
- Do you need a financial buffer?
- Do you need to replace the well spouse's income, so they can take time off work to care for the sick spouse and family for a time?

Total and permanent disablement (TPD)

If you become permanently disabled due to a severe accident or illness and are diagnosed as never able to work again, this type of insurance will give you a lump-sum payment. In this scenario you are effectively financially 'dead', so the payout usually goes towards items you would cover with life insurance (such as debt reduction, education costs, and the like). As you are still alive, of course, items such as funeral expenses or bequests can usually be omitted. There is usually a minimum three-month period before payment so the disability can be verified as permanent. This type of insurance is usually inexpensive and is a great fall-back cover if you are unable to afford defined illness insurances, such as trauma protection.

CASE STUDY

Iosefa and **Sefina** found that they got to the end of each month with just enough money to live. Iosefa worked as a bank teller, and because their two children were at school, Sefina was also able to work, providing a much-needed second income. They sought advice from an insurance broker and agreed they needed a full protection plan. They took out a life insurance policy, as it was not only the cheapest but also where they thought their greatest risk lay. Unfortunately, Iosefa was in a car accident that seriously damaged his spine, and while the bank kindly paid his wages for a few months, they eventually had to let him go. He received treatment and rehabilitation paid for by ACC, and yet he remained confined to his bed for long periods of time.

Three months later Iosefa was advised that a return to his old job was unlikely to happen. While he was likely to receive some support through the government, this would not pay the mortgage and fund the family's day-to-day costs. Had he taken out a total and permanent disablement policy, this would have perhaps provided a freehold home for the family and allowed Sefina's income to pay the day-to-day expenses.

Life insurance

This is for when you depart this world too soon or are diagnosed with a terminal illness. Usually referred to as life insurance, it is a lump-sum (tax-free) payment to the policy owner (or joint owner, if the policy is jointly owned). It could be used to eliminate any debts you leave behind, pay off your mortgage, cover funeral costs, pay for the future education of your children or provide an income for your spouse and family.

There are two main types of life insurance:

- *Term life* — the most common cover found in New Zealand. It provides a set amount of cover for a set period and is cheaper than an endowment policy because there is no investment component. If, however, you cease paying the premiums, the cover ceases.
- *Endowment* and *whole of life* — these have higher premiums because they have a savings component to them. I am not a big fan of these policies because insurance and investment are quite different, and I don't believe they work well in the same product. They are, however, rarely sold today.

CASE STUDY

Philip and **Pamela** and their three young children were living a comfortable life. They had a lovely house in the country, Philip had a great job with a good salary and Pamela ran a part-time business from home. One day, at the young age of 43, Philip had a sudden heart attack and died. They had life cover in place, but unfortunately it was only enough to just cover the mortgage. Pamela, faced with her own grief and looking after three small children who had just lost their father, was struggling to pay the day-to-day living costs. Unless she got the business running again, they would have to downsize the family home.

Pamela now regretted that she hadn't taken the advice of their insurance advisor and increased the amount of Philip's life insurance to cover some additional income until the family was older and she was able to build her business income to cover the family costs.

Considerations for both total & permanent disability and life insurance:

- Might the death or financial death of the income earners result in the loss of vital household income?
- What level of income does the household need to maintain in the absence of one or both incomes?
- How long would this need to be provided (e.g. until your children start or leave school)?
- Would the survivor need to employ children's daycare, housekeeper or nanny services beyond what is presently required?
- Would the surviving spouse continue working (if presently working), or return to work (if not)? If not, for how long, and what income is needed to survive this period?
- Might there be any expenditure required, such as asset purchases, upgrades or alterations? (An example could be purchasing a freehold home for the family, or putting down a house deposit.)
- With any of the above, would you sell any assets to self-insure for the above (thus allowing you to not have to purchase insurance to cover)? An example would be the cashing in of liquid assets, such as bank or term deposits or a share portfolio.

'Have you ever met a widow who thought her husband was over-insured?'

— ANON

BUSINESS INSURANCE

This is a very specialist area, so I am not going to go into any detail other than to say if you have a business you need to talk to an insurance advisor who specialises in business risk. The types of cover include:

- general insurance
- business asset insurance
- business interruption insurance
- indemnity insurance
- commercial vehicle insurance
- key person insurance
- shareholder insurance

Even if you are a sole trader or have a side hustle it is important to understand if you need any of the above types of insurance. You do not want to be in a situation where your claim is turned down because your personal insurance policy has exclusions if, for example, you used your car or home for your business.

Money-saving tips

There are various ways to save money on your insurances.

- Increase the level of your excess (house/contents/vehicle/ medical insurance).
- Fit smoke and burglar alarms; this will usually get you a discount on your home and contents insurance.
- You will often get a discount if you have all of your insurances with one company.
- If you can it is usually cheaper to pay your insurances annually as monthly premiums incur a finance cost.

- When making a claim check that what you get paid out is worth more than the cost of losing any no-claims bonus.
- Shop around and compare different policies: some companies offer discounts for a range of criteria, for which you may qualify. This is not easy to do, so consider using an insurance advisor who will not only do this for you but will understand the nuances of the various policies.
- Extend the waiting period or stand-down period on your income protection from one month to a longer period of two to six months. First, though, ensure you have funds in place to cover your expenses during this waiting period. This is where your emergency fund comes in handy.
- Don't leave it too long before taking out personal insurance. If you have any health issues your insurance costs can increase, your cover can be limited, or in some cases you might not be able to get any cover. I know when you are young you think that nothing will happen to you, but you will be amazed at what can!
- Insurance premiums can increase dramatically as you age, and it can be tempting to cancel your policy. The older you get, however, the more likely you are to have health issues and need your cover. Talk to your insurance advisor about whether level premiums are for you. This is where the premiums you pay are higher at the beginning, but they don't increase, or increase very little, over time. It's a cost-effective option if you think you'll be paying insurance over a long period.
- Review your insurances regularly to make sure you have the most appropriate cover for your current situation. As a rule of thumb, as your net worth increases, the need for life insurance decreases.
- Advice can save you money. Without it you may end up

over-insured in one area and under-insured in another, which may result in more costly premiums or be more costly at claim time when you find out you weren't covered for what you thought.

- When applying for insurance tell the truth as if you leave out important information you risk your claim not being paid.
- Most importantly save, as the more you build up your wealth, the less reliant you are on insurance because you are more able to self-insure.

If you think insurance is expensive — try paying the claim.'

– ANON

Did you know?

The top five causes of death are:

- Neoplasms (cancer)
- Cardiovascular diseases
- Self-harm and interpersonal violence
- Transport injuries
- Diabetes and kidney diseases

The biggest risks contributing to death, disability and ill health are tobacco, high body mass index and high blood pressure.
"Couple" in the table refers to the risk of either party dying.

Risks you face as a non-smoker			
Risk	**Male**	**Female**	**Couple**
Dying	9%	6%	15%
Becoming totally and permanently disabled	4%	4%	9%
Suffering a critical illness	17%	11%	26%
Becoming temporarily disabled	10%	19%	28%

Risks you face as a smoker			
Risk	**Male**	**Female**	**Couple**
Dying	17%	12%	27%
Becoming totally and permanently disabled	4%	4%	8%
Suffering a critical illness	32%	25%	49%
Becoming temporarily disabled	9%	18%	25%

Source: Quality Product Research

Managing your affairs

There's an old saying that the two certainties in life are death and taxes. It follows that at some stage someone is going to have to look after your affairs. Modern family structures and lifestyles mean that estate planning is crucial to lessen the financial and emotional burdens on the people you care about when unplanned events happen.

WILL

A key place to start is to get a will, which a surprising number of New Zealanders do not have. It might be because they might think they are too young to need one, assume their family or partner already knows their wishes, don't think they are important, just don't want to think about dying, or simply it just hasn't occurred to them. A will gives instructions as to what will happen after your death, including:

- It gives instructions for the distribution of your assets.
- It names your beneficiaries (the people who will benefit from your estate) and sets out which of your possessions and other property you want them to receive.
- It names a guardian or guardians for your children.
- It specifies your funeral arrangements.
- It is legally binding and comes into effect when you die and is the only way you can ensure your assets are distributed according to your wishes.
- You can appoint an executor who will look after your property and administer your estate after your death.
- To make a valid will, you must be of sound mind and over 18 years of age. It must be in writing and witnessed by two people who are not beneficiaries and are over 18 years of age.

- You can alter and rewrite your will as many times as you like.

If you don't have a will, you die *intestate* and your wishes may not be carried out. Instead, your assets will be distributed in accordance with the Administration Act 1969, regardless of what you would have wanted. If you are young, it still makes sense to have a will so your family are clear about your wishes should something unexpected happen. Once you accumulate a few assets, get married or have a long-term partner and have children, a will is essential. Your will should be updated regularly or after major life changes, such as:

- getting married — marriage automatically revokes (cancels) your previous will
- entering into a de facto relationship
- getting divorced
- having children
- purchasing or selling major assets
- setting up a family trust

CASE STUDY

Maria passed away in her late sixties and although she had an up-to-date will, it wasn't overly specific. She had provided instructions on how her property was to be distributed but had failed to mention anything about her funeral or where she was to be buried. Before she passed away, she had mentioned that she didn't want a funeral. Naturally the family thought there should be one, but a heated discussion followed about the details. Some wanted a church ceremony, while others disagreed as she hadn't been at all religious. Then they argued over whether she should be cremated or buried. They finally agreed to have her cremated but then they couldn't decide where to put her ashes: with her husband (whom she didn't like very much in the later stages of their marriage), or next to her family? A decision couldn't be reached, and she ended up in an urn at the house of one family member. Sadly, it created so much stress and animosity that some family members didn't talk to others for many years.

Although these seem simple decisions, at such an emotional time they can create an enormous amount of stress and friction if your wishes are not clear. You never know what is going to happen tomorrow. If you plan responsibly for your future, you will have peace of mind knowing that you are making it easier for your loved ones to carry out your wishes at the end of your life's journey.

POWER OF ATTORNEY — ANTICIPATE THE UNEXPECTED

There are many instances when not being able to manage your own affairs could have serious consequences for you or your family, which could result in financial loss. Incapacity through illness or accident can happen for a wide variety of reasons at any time and at any age. You could also be 'incapacitated' in the sense that you are unable to act on your own affairs if you went overseas for business or decided to travel. In your absence, some urgent matter, such as signing sale documents for your property, may be required. Covid has fast-tracked the use of digital signatures, but they are still not universally accepted.

A power of attorney is a legal document enabling you to appoint a person or organisation (the 'attorney') to act on your behalf when you cannot. Unlike a will, which is activated on death, powers of attorney have relevance only when you are alive. As long as you are capable of doing so, you can cancel or change the conditions of your powers of attorney at any time.

There are two main types of power of attorney:

- *General* — A general power of attorney applies only during temporary absences from New Zealand or temporary physical incapacity.
- *Enduring* — There are two types of enduring power of attorney: one is for matters relating to property (assets), the other for personal care and welfare (e.g. accommodation, or medical decisions).

You can appoint an individual (or more than one) and/or an organisation to act on your behalf only if you become mentally incapable. Alternatively, you can arrange for a power of attorney to come into effect while you are of sound mind and continue to apply if you become mentally incapable. You can stipulate in these documents whether you wish to place limitations on the authority (e.g. only in respect of certain property, or for a certain time), if a successor attorney should be appointed, and/ or if the attorney should consult with a third party, such as a nominated doctor.

Only an individual over 20 years of age can be appointed as your personal care and welfare attorney. Typically, it would be a family member or friend that you trust implicitly to look after your best interests. Some people have a 'backup' in case their attorney dies or can't perform the role. An example might be appointing your partner as attorney and a close family friend as a 'backup'. For your property attorney, the same would apply, except that you can appoint an organisation (e.g. a lawyer or trust company) to be your attorney. If you feel that your family or friends would not act impartially and in your best interests, or that they would not have the time or expertise to manage your affairs properly, using a professional attorney would be preferable.

If you are unable to act on your affairs for any reason and you don't have enduring powers of attorney, no one can step in and manage your affairs without first applying to the Family Court. In the interim, until someone is appointed by the Family Court, your financial position could be severely affected, which may result in personal financial loss. If, for example, you had a business and were the sole signatory, no one else would be empowered to sign on your behalf and this could have consequences for your business, your staff, and others.

CASE STUDY

Harry was 87 years old with a number of health issues. His mental health was also starting to suffer. It was becoming more challenging by the day for his wife to look after him. Sandra, who was of a similar age to Harry, decided she really couldn't care for him properly and talked to him about going into a care facility. Needless to say, Harry wasn't very impressed and swore he was not going to leave his home. Eventually Sandra had to make the decision to get a court order to put him in the home. Not only was this a costly exercise, it was also stressful. If Harry had a personal care and welfare enduring power of attorney in place, a doctor's certificate would have enabled Sandra to make the decision to get Harry the professional care he needed.

Enduring powers of attorney and wills are essential documents as they reduce the risks you could face. They are easy to prepare and are a quick and inexpensive way of having proper legal plans in place for the ongoing management of your affairs. Discuss your options with your lawyer or a public trustee company, such as the Public Trust, Perpetual Guardian or Trustee Executors.

FUNERAL TRUSTS — LIGHTENING THE BURDEN FOR THOSE LEFT BEHIND

If you are concerned about not having enough funds in your estate, a funeral trust puts money aside to pay for your funeral expenses. It spares your loved ones any additional stress and anxiety and reassures them that the costs of your funeral will be covered to the amount set aside in your funeral plan.

You can choose how much you want to set aside to cover your funeral. The funds for your funeral are invested until they are needed to pay for your funeral expenses. They cannot be withdrawn within your lifetime but are available as soon as your funeral expenses need paying.

There are basically two main options for putting money aside for a funeral:

- *Savings plan*: this is a drip-feed option where you put aside a monthly amount until you reach the amount you want to set aside. Typically, people in their forties or fifties go for this option as they have more time.
- *Lump sum*: this is based on your current age and how much you want to set aside. This option is mainly used by those over 65.

A quick internet search will show you who can provide these for you.

FAMILY TRUSTS — PLANNING FOR TODAY AND TOMORROW

Many people are concerned that their assets — real estate, motor vehicles, valuable artworks or household items, company shares — will be lost to unwanted claims, either while they are alive or through their estate when they die. Trusts are one of the oldest legal structures used to protect beneficiaries and assets. They can offer greater estate planning flexibility and protection than a will.

A family trust is a legal arrangement where the trustees (as legal owners of the assets) hold assets for the benefit of beneficiaries as set out in the trust deed. A trust deed allows you to still have some control over, and get the benefit of, these assets. The primary purpose of a trust is to safeguard assets for future generations (while you are alive and after you die) by:

- protecting against professional liability claims; employers and businesses can face a high risk of substantial fines and criminal penalties under various legislation
- retaining control of assets after you die (e.g. your trustees can spread a child's inheritance over a number of years)
- safeguarding your assets from financial disaster
- preparing for possible capital gains or death taxes
- maintaining confidentiality about your financial affairs
- preparing for the time you might need residential care planning
- protecting assets against unexpected business debts
- reducing the risk of future partners making relationship property claims (the court has limited power to interfere with trusts formed prior to a relationship being entered into)
- gaining tax advantages (in certain circumstances)

Here's an example of what one person might do to put in place a series of protections.

CASE STUDY

Anneke is a director of a company that leases a building. She has had to give a personal guarantee on the lease, but this is limited to the equivalent of three months' rental. Her company shares and house are owned by a family trust established to protect her and her children. The company leases certain large items of plant and equipment from the family trust. Anneke doesn't generally give personal guarantees to suppliers. A personal salary is paid to her and dividends for extra profit are paid to the trust. If Anneke suffered a business setback, she is in a better position to retain enough assets to start again and still keep a roof over her family.

Family trusts are very prevalent in New Zealand. There is an increasing level of regulation applied to trusts which is making them more costly to maintain and many are being unwound as a result. It is essential that a trust is properly administered, that records are kept, and that the trust assets are dealt with according to the terms of the trust otherwise they will not offer the protection they were set up for.

RELATIONSHIP PROPERTY

One of the main reasons relationships break up is over money. Getting on the same page as your partner when it comes to how you manage your money is often not an easy task. Although tough, it is prudent to have those conversations early in the relationship so you prevent potential issues down the track. Relationships can be complex financially because we:

- are starting families later in life
- may have had significant previous relationships
- may have our own assets that have different values from our new partner
- may have children from previous relationships. The Property (Relationships Act) 1976 provides that if a couple has been married or in a de facto relationship for three years or more, all property they own individually is deemed to be relationship property, not separate property, i.e. it is owned equally (unless there are exceptional circumstances). The definition of de facto relationship is very broad and you do not have to be living together.

If you do not want to face the prospect of splitting all of your combined assets in half in the unfortunate event of the relationship ending after three years, you need to formally contract out of the Act. Sometimes known as a pre-nuptial or pre-nup, this agreement sets out what each party brings into the relationship and how assets will be divided when the relationship terminates. Both parties must get legal advice for this agreement to be valid. It is important to note that if you have assets in a trust this doesn't necessarily mean they are exempt from being classified as relationship property so seek specialist legal advice. It is a simple legal process but the conversations with your partner may not be. Ideally you want to have these conversations well before the three years to give yourselves time to work through any potential issues. If you are struggling with these conversations, it may mean you are not overly aligned financially with your partner and could be a warning sign of future challenges!

Case Study: Bouncing back from a financial disaster (Dawn — Hamilton)

It was a mistake that first got me really thinking about money. After I finished university studies, I got my first job and managed to build up a tidy sum of seven or eight thousand in my savings account. I did some research and decided to invest it in a finance company at 9% return. This sounds highly dubious to me now, but it wasn't uncommon at the time, and the company somehow had a solid 'investment grade' rating.

Roll on another year or two, and Bridgecorp went thoroughly bust in the 2007–8 sharemarket crash. I remember thinking at the time, 'This sucks, but at least it's just money.' Easier to say in my twenties than the unlucky people who invested more and later in their life, of course.

It also was the catalyst for me realising I needed to learn more about investing. I proceeded to read every book I could find on the topic, absorbing small gems from each such as the value of sinking funds, tracking net worth regularly, and when you shouldn't invest in finance companies. I also came across the Mr. Money Mustache website, and while the investment amounts discussed on the website often dwarfed mine, the concept of investing in low-fee index funds with the aim of future freedom was an eye-opener.

My partner and I have always worked part-time in order to have some time for creative pursuits and our young daughter. This worked well from a lifestyle perspective but meant we were late in terms of buying our own home. Ten years on from the Bridgecorp incident, we finally found a house and made an offer just one dollar under the existing government grant cap. Thanks to slow steady investing, KiwiSaver, the grant, and working a few more hours, we had built up a 21% deposit and scraped enough together for a mortgage. It was a good feeling to manage that ourselves and have somewhere to live where we were allowed a compost heap!

I still have plenty to learn, and I don't know if I'll manage to retire particularly early, but I appreciate that knowledge and investments can open doors and create options. Good investments, that is.

In a Nutshell
- Thinking about and planning for life's risks is a vital part of your financial plan.
- Decide which risks you want to take on yourself and which you want to pass on to an insurance company.
- Get good professional advice to ensure you have the best cover for your circumstances and so you are neither under- nor over-insured.
- Review your insurances regularly to ensure they are always fit for purpose.
- Consider what estate planning you need (wills, powers of attorney, trusts, etc.) to help manage and protect your future.

Achieving success

NOW WE HAVE ALMOST REACHED the end of the book, let's put some more focus on how to stay on track to give you the best chance to succeed in your journey towards financial success and more financial freedom.

Success

If you look in the dictionary for the meaning of the word success, you will find that it is *the achievement of one's goal or aim.* So, basically, anyone can achieve success by simply achieving their aim or goal.

For me success is about being excited about getting out of bed each day, leading a fulfilling life, and one with few regrets. It is also about having the freedom to do what I choose. In the most part I have achieved this; however, the reality is that some days I just do not want to get out of bed and on others I am overwhelmed with all that I need to do. I have been particularly successful financially, although it hasn't come without its challenges, and it has taken a lot of focus and determination and a fair bit of delayed gratification. Importantly I put a lot of thought into what a successful life would look like for me many years ago. I developed financial goals, which I reviewed regularly, around that vision and put a plan in place to build the life I wanted. For the most part I have achieved my definition of what a successful life would be.

What does success mean to you? How do you know when you have achieved it? How will you measure it? It is not necessarily important to measure it, but you don't want to be living a life where you are constantly chasing the illusion of success. You may beat yourself up because you haven't been successful, but ironically you don't know what success means to you! Often success is measured in small things that make you feel good rather than one grandiose thing. Your definition will also probably change over time. What does success for you look like?

_____

_____

_____

_____

_____

30% knowing what you want

+

30% positive self-image

+

30% attitude that you can do it

+

10% technical know-how

=

Financial Success

Learn

Learning is a key part of your financial journey. It keeps your mind engaged and active, and you get new knowledge-based perspectives on the world around you. It helps you gain new experiences, trains your brain to handle a wide range of challenges, and keeps your neural pathways active. Many studies cite that learning new skills is an incredible way to improve your life. It can certainly improve your finances. When we succeed in learning something we feel better and are more confident in ourselves and our ability to tackle all sorts of new tasks and make good decisions. Learning can help improve your mental health and reduce stress. It can also be a great deal of fun learning new skills and talents and meeting different people along the way. A huge number of benefits can be derived from a life of learning.

There are unlimited ways you can learn, many of them free or at little cost: books, the internet, courses, friends and family, professional advisors, or just getting out there and experiencing life. Do be mindful, though, of the source of your information as there is a lot that is incorrect and misleading. If you are open to learning, there are opportunities all around you to expand your mind.

Visualisation

The 'law of attraction' is a belief that you attract into your life what you believe and think about. The theory is that whatever consumes your thoughts is what you will eventually get in life, whether positive or negative. Visualisation essentially helps you put the law of attraction into place. It is the practice of imagining what you want to achieve in the future as if it were true today. The process of visualising directs your subconscious to be aware of the end goal you have in mind. People around the world have been using various kinds of visualisation techniques, meditations, and prayers for centuries. It often gets a bad reputation as being too fluffy and not grounded in reality. However, everybody from professional sportspeople to successful businesspeople is using and benefitting from some form of visualisation technique. It can provide you with a compass, adding direction to your journey. Without it, you may struggle to see your potential as you get caught up in day-to-day life.

Visualisation is both envisioning what you want in the future along with imagining every step towards your desired outcome. It can strengthen your motivation and helps you to feel excited to create your dream life. It helps to program your brain and makes you feel more confident. The more that you are visualising yourself achieving your goals and dreams, the more it anchors in your brain and the more confident you can start to feel. It can help with stress because when are visualising, you are normally in a calm state which can help clear your mind, eliminating any worries and stresses you may have. Here are some tips:

- Try not to overthink things, otherwise you may get lost in the detail.
- Incorporate all of your senses in the process.
- Make sure you are calm and relaxed.
- Create a vision board of images representing what you want to achieve.
- Have a regular visualisation practice.
- Connect with the emotion of what you are visualising.
- Visualise with a sense of knowing and certainty.

While the law of attraction may not be an immediate solution for all of life's challenges, it can help you learn to cultivate a more optimistic outlook on life, which leads to many benefits. It may also help you stay motivated to continue working towards your goals.

'The future belongs to those who believe in the beauty of their dreams.'
—ELEANOR ROOSEVELT

Good people

Having support and help from others will be an important component of your success. It could be your life partner, a friend or family member, professional advisor, or you might be part of a group that provides learning and support to each other. Everyone needs help and guidance.

You do, however, need to be mindful about where you get financial help, professional or otherwise. I am a member of a few finance- and investment-related Facebook groups and while it is wonderful to see how generous and supportive people are sharing their experience to help others, I do question the knowledge behind some of the advice. The challenge is that the questions posted are often brief so a lot of important information can be left out. A professional advisor will spend a lot of time understanding the person and their issues before giving any advice. So please use a filter when considering what you are reading online. Context and knowledge are critically important. Forums can be great for getting very specific advice like 'I need to get a new roof on my house, what questions should I be asking the roofer?', or 'Can you recommend some good budgeting apps?' Questions like 'What KiwiSaver fund should I be in?' or 'Do I need life insurance?' are best posed to a suitably qualified professional.

It might also be that your friends are better at helping you with motivation and focus but you would be best to get more technical advice from someone suitably qualified to give it. If you do decide to get professional advice, not all advisors are created equal so you will need to put effort into finding one that best suits your needs. You could ask your friends who are good with money, or search the internet, or ask other advisors you might have (such as your accountant) for recommendations. You may end up working with your advisors for a number of years, so doing some homework will pay off. Here are some questions that will be helpful finding a good advisor:

- What qualifications do you hold?
- What is your role with the company and who owns it?
- How long have you been involved in your field?
- What practical and professional experience do you have?
- What industry bodies or associations do you belong to?
- What are your other services and their associated fees?

TIPS FOR GETTING THE MOST OUT OF AN ADVISOR

- Make sure you feel comfortable and at ease with them. Having a good rapport with them is vital and will make communication more effective.
- Be open and honest. What you tell them is in confidence; and the more they know, the better they can advise you. Leaving out critical information can make a difference to how good the advice is.
- Get clear on the outcomes you want to achieve and communicate them to your advisor.

- Give feedback; your advisors are not mind-readers.
- Be realistic. No matter how good an advisor is, they may not be able to sort all your issues out in an hour or two.
- Advice is only good if you act upon it. If you don't like the advice or don't feel right about it, do some more research. Just because you don't like what the advisor has told you to do, it doesn't mean the advice is not good.

I cannot stress how important it is to get help from someone who knows what they are doing. If you look at financially successful people, you'll see they all work with a highly qualified team of experts who have helped them get where they are today. I am not suggesting that you assemble a huge team around you when you are starting out, but the reality is that it is unlikely that you will have all the skills you need to achieve everything you want.

Check-ups

Your finances don't manage themselves and they need to be monitored and reviewed on a regular basis — just like you take your car to get a warrant, or you visit the dentist or the doctor for check-ups. I think either the beginning of the calendar year or the beginning of the financial year is a good time to do a financial review to ensure you are on track to achieve your goals and dreams. If you have developed good systems, this review should be relatively painless and take very little time. Here are some questions to ask yourself when doing your review:

- If you have consumer debt, how are you tracking getting it paid off?
- Are you being smart with the money you earn and are you spending it wisely?

- Is there a positive gap between what you are earning and spending?
- Is your money system working effectively?
- Are you happy with how you are managing your money or are there improvements that can be made?
- How much has your net worth improved by?
- How much do you still owe on your mortgage? Can you pay more off your mortgage so you save interest and get your mortgage paid off sooner?
- Have you got the correct mortgage structure for your current situation?
- Are you receiving all the government benefits to which you're entitled?
- Is your estate planning up to date? Is your will current and do you have powers of attorney in place?
- Have you reviewed your insurances to ensure you have the best cover for where you are today?
- Do you have copies of all of your important documents?
- Are your advisors still meeting your needs?
- Have you done your last year's accounts and/or checked to see if you are due a tax refund?
- Do you have a savings or investment plan in place and has it been reviewed recently?
- Have you checked your KiwiSaver balance and are you still in the most appropriate fund?
- How are you tracking towards providing for yourself in retirement?
- Have you set your new goals for the coming year?

After you have reviewed your finances, remember the most important part — take action to make the necessary changes.

Keep the faith

There may be times when you find it all too hard and you wish you had never committed to taking control of your finances and becoming a good money manager. You wouldn't be human if you didn't have these feelings. However, the most important thing is that you keep taking those small steps every day. You will be surprised how, over time, even the smallest change makes a big difference.

TIPS FOR KEEPING ON TRACK

Here are nine tips that may help you stay on track:

1. Don't panic

This is the cardinal rule in all situations when it all gets a bit much. Take a deep breath and don't make any rash decisions. Maybe take a walk or talk to a friend or partner about what you find difficult. Often when we look at things later, after we have had a break and have a clearer head, they don't seem as bad. Remember — 90% of what we worry about never happens!

2. Remember your vision

Visualise how you will feel when you do become a good money manager, your money system is up and running efficiently, and you feel that you are at last in control of your finances. Imagine yourself achieving your dreams.

'Whether you believe you can do something, or don't believe, either way you are right.'
—HENRY FORD

3. Find some help

Who can you talk to? Everyone needs someone to talk to. I often recommend to couples that they set aside some time, either every week or month, to talk through their finances. This means they spend focused, quality time on it, rather than have lots of ineffectual conversations when they're in the middle of doing other things. If you are single, find a friend that you can do this exercise with. If you have a professional advisor, use them as a sounding board. Remember: a problem shared is a problem halved.

4. Don't look back

Worrying about things that have happened won't achieve anything apart from wasting energy. Or as one of my good friends says, 'The only thing you get from looking at the past is a sore neck.' You need your energy focusing on tackling more positive activities and moving ahead.

5. Don't beat yourself up

We are human and we all make mistakes. This is how we learn. Often, it's the most successful people who have made the most mistakes.

Did you know? Albert Einstein experienced more failures than any scientist of his time; however, he also achieved more successes.

6. Damage control

It something does go pear-shaped ask yourself: what in particular went wrong? Understand the issues, learn from the experience, and think about what you need to do to get back on track. Then calmly go about putting the changes in place.

7. Take action

Remember that success comes one step at a time. Keep stepping forward no matter how small those steps might be.

8. Reassess

Sometimes when you get off track it's because your goals are not quite right for you any more. Check in with your original goals. Are they still applicable or do they need some tweaking?

9. Be patient

There are no short cuts or quick, simple ways to make you rich overnight. Follow the basic principles outlined throughout this book and you will have a financially comfortable retirement. Remember — time is one of your most powerful tools.

'You will never change your life until you change something you do daily. The secret of your success is found in your daily routine.'
—JOHN MAXWELL

Case Study: Trusting your instincts and focusing on your goals (Christina — Wellington)

I have bought and sold three houses in the past six years. This wasn't exactly planned, but it is just how things panned out.

After my divorce, I found myself renting and then flatting again. Both were fine because they were necessary steps for me to set myself up again financially.

I went flatting with a woman who I thought was a friend. Unfortunately, things did not work out and I soon found myself living in a house and having to cover the entire rent for it. I was able to manage this as I was earning a sufficient income as a contractor. Things took another unexpected turn not long before my lease was due to expire. I received a phone call from the homeowner informing me that she had just broken up from her boyfriend and would need her house back. Finding myself without a home, I contacted a friend to ask if I could rent her spare bedroom.

For some time I had been paddling with a couple of friends who told me about a small beach township where house prices were still very reasonable. One of my friends was an architect, who pointed out the houses were better oriented for the sun than the suburb where he and I lived. I decided to act on their opinion and started my hunt for a home. Before too long I found the ideal place. It was very small and humble, but I could afford to buy it outright with my divorce settlement, so I did.

An opportunity then came up for me to go abroad and complete a master's degree. While I was away, I decided to sell that little half house and it turned a tidy little profit. I intentionally placed all of the proceeds of the sale into savings and vowed never to touch it no matter what. When I returned to New Zealand it took me some time to find paid employment but I stuck to my word.

As a result, I eventually had enough saved up to buy another home in that same area, but this time a larger house with four bedrooms. My job at that stage required a fair amount of travel and the frequent airport connections made the location of my house untenable.

When Covid panic hit in 2020, my gut instinct told me there would be 'bargains' as people looked to sell up and reduce their mortgages. I soon spotted an apartment for sale close to the airport and put in an offer which took every last dollar I had. I bought the apartment just as the property market went crazy for sellers. As with my first tiny home, I made a tidy profit.

The lesson of the story for me was to trust my instincts. The beach township where I bought my first property was a bit rough, but I chose a house with extraordinary views and phenomenal afternoon sun. I made myself a promise not to touch my capital after I sold that property no matter how tempted I was, and that decision allowed me to purchase my first proper house for myself. I then trusted my instinct that the turmoil caused by Covid would make it a good time to buy a property that in normal times would have been out of my price bracket.

In a Nutshell
- Define what success means to you. It will provide you with a compass for your financial journey.
- Visualise what you want to achieve with all of your being.
- Surround yourself with good people.
- Check in on your progress regularly and change your goals when needed.
- Keep the faith. When things become difficult, take a deep breath, work out the problem, and then take a step forward.
- Believe in the beauty of your dreams. If do you and you take action, you can achieve all you desire.

About Lisa Dudson

BBS, Dip (Business Management), GradDip (PR), PostGradDipBus (Financial Planning)

Lisa began investing when she was just 16 years old. She brings unrivalled passion and enthusiasm to her clients, drawing on her experience as an investor, author, entrepreneur and professional speaker to provide pragmatic and meaningful advice. She is a director and shareholder of Saturn Advice and National Capital and provides financial and property advice through Acumen.

Her wealth of expertise has seen Lisa featured as a media commentator on financial issues. She has written articles for numerous publications including the *New Zealand Herald*, *Sunday Star-Times*, *Woman's Day*, *Yahoo!* and the *NZ Property Magazine*, and has appeared on various radio and TV shows including *The AM Show*, *Breakfast*, *Good Morning*, *60 Minutes* and TV1 and TV3 News.

Lisa is also a best-selling author of:
The New Zealand Money Guide
The New Zealand Property Guide
Money & You

Winning the Money War
Create Wealth
Get Your Head out of the Sand
The Complete Guide to Residential Property Investment in
New Zealand

Today she loves nothing more than helping people grow their wealth through the identification of financial goals and astute, informed decision-making. In her spare time Lisa is an avid traveller, having been to over 70 countries, and enjoys yoga, tennis and the gym.

www.acumen.co.nz
www.nationalcapital.co.nz
www.saturnadvice.co.nz

Need Some Financial Help?

Whether you are concerned about your future retirement or living a better lifestyle right now, you'll be amazed at what a difference the right financial guidance can make. Knowing you're on the right financial path dramatically decreases your stress levels and, more importantly, can save you thousands.

MONEY BUYS YOU FREEDOM

I provide an experienced financial sounding board to help you achieve more clarity and direction on how to change and improve your financial life and buy you more freedom. Irrespective of your current income, I can help you build a solid financial base and determine a clear strategy to build and maintain your wealth.

I have spent over two decades working with people to eliminate their financial worries and build their wealth. I can help you too. I can either help you directly or refer you to someone in my team.

Acumen provides financial and property investment guidance via individual personalised consultations. I also offer a programme to help my clients purchase quality investment property by managing the full process for them.
www.acumen.co.nz

National Capital provides free KiwiSaver advice. We are paid a service fee by the KiwiSaver providers so there is no advice fee to you. We research all the main funds and provide independent advice.
www.nationalcapital.co.nz

Saturn Advice is a financial advisory and investment planning firm providing impartial advice. We are not aligned to any fund manager or broker and our staff are paid fixed remuneration, not commissions. In a market dominated by big, vertically integrated financial services companies this is unique. It is a relief to be able to refer my clients to a non-conflicted financial advice business where your interests will be put first. It's important.
www.saturnadvice.co.nz

You can access a bunch of free stuff here:
www.acumen.co.nz/free-stuff/

Index

Exercises

Case studies